NEW PEOPLE STRATEGIES FOR
THE BRITISH ARMED FORCES

NEW PEOPLE STRATEGIES FOR THE BRITISH ARMED FORCES

Editors

Alex Alexandrou, Richard Bartle
and
Richard Holmes

FRANK CASS
LONDON • PORTLAND, OR

First Published in 2002 in Great Britain by
FRANK CASS PUBLISHERS
Crown House, 47 Chase Side, Southgate,
London, N14 5BP, England

and in the United States of America by
FRANK CASS PUBLISHERS
c/o ISBS 5824, N.E. Hassalo Street
Portland, Oregon 97213-3644

*Website:*www.frankcass.com

British Library Cataloguing in Publication Data

New people strategies for the British armed forces
1. Great Britain. Army – Personnel mangement
I. Alexandrou, Alex II. Bartle, Richard III. Holmes,
Richard, 1946–
355.6'1'0941

ISBN 0-7146-5212-1 (cloth)
ISBN 0-7146-8202-0 (paper)

Library of Congress Cataloging-in-Publication Data

Alexandrou, Alex.
New people strategies for the British armed forces/Alex
Alexandrou, Richard Bartle and Richard Holmes.
p.cm.
ISBN 0-7146-5212-1 (hbk.) ISBN 0-7146-8202-0 (pbk.)
1. Great Britain – Armed Forces – Personnel management.
I.Bartle, Richard. II. Holmes, Richard. III. Title.
UB57 .A74 2001
355'.00941'09051–dc21

2001005872

Typeset in Palatino in 10.5/13pt by FiSH Books, London.
Printed in Great Britain by MPG Books Ltd., Bodmin, Cornwall

Contents

The Authors

Introduction

The Authors

Alex Alexandrou has worked extensively in the field of industrial relations and human resource management, particularly in the public sector. He is now a Cranfield University lecturer in the Department of Defence Management and Security Analysis at the Royal Military College of Science, specialising in HRM from a public sector perspective. He is the co-editor of two recent books on HRM in the Armed Forces.

Richard Bartle was an Army Officer for 23 years. He retired in the rank of Lieutenant Colonel and is now a Cranfield University lecturer in the Department of Defence Management and Security Analysis at the Royal Military College of Science (RMCS). He has published widely on Organisational Behaviour and Human Resource Management in the military sphere and is the co-editor of two recent books on HRM in the Armed Forces.

Peter Caddick-Adams is a lecturer in Military and Security Studies at the Security Studies Institute, RMCS. He is the author of *By God They Can Fight* (1995) and numerous articles on military history, especially the Territorial Army. During 1996–97 he served as the official SHAPE historian covering operations in Bosnia and is now working on a military history of Yugoslavia.

Gerald Frost is a journalist who has written widely about domestic and international politics. He has been Director of the Centre for Policy Studies and head of the Institute for European Defence and Strategic Studies which he founded in 1981. He has edited more than 70 books and monographs as well as several collections of essays including *Not Fit to Fight: The Cultural Subversion of the Armed Forces in Britain and America*; *Europe in Turmoil: The Struggle for Pluralism* and *Loyalty Misplaced: Misdirected Virtue and Social Disintegration*.

Richard Holmes is Professor of Military and Security Studies at Cranfield University, Royal Military College of Science. He has written a number of books including *Firing Line* and has recently edited *The Oxford Companion to Military History*. He regularly writes and presents television documentaries: his BBC 2 series *The Western Front* was screened in the summer of 1999. Until late 2000 he was Director of Reserve Forces and Cadets in the MoD.

Caroline Kennedy-Pipe is Professor of International Relations in the Department of Politics at the University of Sheffield. She is the author of *Russia and the World* published by Edward Arnold (1998), the Editor of the Journal *Civil Wars* and author of a number of pieces on women and war.

Patrick Mileham completed the MPhil in International Relations at Cambridge while serving in the Royal Tank Regiment. He is now Reader in Management Studies at the University of Paisley, Scotland.

Jerry Plant joined the Royal Navy in 1979. He read Engineering at the Royal Naval Engineering College and recently completed an MDA at Cranfield University, RMCS. Currently he holds the rank of Commander and works as a consultant with the Director of Management and Consultancy Services providing business analysis and job evaluation techniques to the MoD. He is interested in the application of commercial HRM practices within the military environment.

Allan Ross was commissioned in the Royal Air Force in 1982. He retired in the rank of Squadron Leader before taking up a post with the Royal Saudi Arabian Air Force. He is now a lecturer in law at Cranfield University in the Department of Defence Management and Security Analysis where he specialises in the impact of national and EC law on the military.

Hew Strachan is Professor of Modern History and Director of the Scottish Centre for War Studies, University of Glasgow. He is joint editor of *War in History* and was Lees Knowles

Lecturer, Trinity College, Cambridge, in 1995. His books include *European Armies and the Conduct of War*; *Tactics, Technology and the British Army 1815–1854*; *The Politics of the British Army* and (as editor) *The British Army, Manpower and Society into the Twenty-First Century*; and *The First World War. Volume 1: To Arms.*

Stephen Welch is a Lecturer in the Department of Politics at the University of Durham. His main interest is in political culture and he has recently written and published on the ethics of International Policing.

Helen Wildman was commissioned into the Army in 1982 and has served in UK, Germany and Hong Kong specialising in developmental education and career management. She has an MSc(Econ) in Strategic Studies from the University of Wales, Aberystwyth, and is now studying for an MDA with Cranfield University. She is currently based in Rheindahlen, where she is responsible for British Army Media Operations throughout Germany.

Introduction

Human Resource Management as a concept for the UK military continues not only to grow in importance but also to tax the minds of both senior management within the three Services, and civil servants and politicians within the Ministry of Defence. Over the last few years we have sought to enhance and stimulate the debate on many of the various strands of military HRM through our publications and conferences.

This book seeks to go beyond merely examining and criticising what has happened to date. Our aim is to put forward new concepts and ideas on a number of subjects and themes that are currently causing concern for the policy makers.

In part some progress has been made since our last book. The Government's recent Spending Review (2000), publication of the updated Defence Policy (2001) and the introduction of a new pay system – Pay 2000, have begun to address some of our concerns. Additionally, in order to conform to European and domestic legislation amendments have been made to the Service Discipline Acts by means of the Armed Forces Discipline Act 2000. The publication of the long awaited Review of Defence Training and Education (2001) has produced some interesting new ideas in this field. Progress has been made by the Defence Committee with its examination of the Strategic Defence Review's Policy for People (1998) and two reports have been published this year covering both Regular and Reserve Forces personnel (2001).

The appointment of Admiral Sir Michael Boyce to succeed General Sir Charles Guthrie as Chief of the Defence Staff has generated much interest not only within the Armed Services but also among the politicians and media. The latter have also latched onto the issue of the creation of a European Army and its subsequent effects on control and manning levels.

This publication will seek to examine how the MoD should tackle a number of issues. These will include the further integration of European and domestic civilian legislation, primarily focusing on the Human Rights Act

1998, recruitment and retention of Regulars and Reservists, the future role of women in the military and whether Armed Forces personnel should have the right to have their views put forward by a representative body. Overlapping these issues, the subjects of culture, morale and the moral component will also be vigorously assessed.

We hope that our book will provide some answers, be informative, stimulate positive debate among both academics and practitioners and, as always, encourage others to research and publish in this area.

Alex Alexandrou
Richard Bartle
Richard Holmes

The 2000 Spending Review and Beyond: The Future Implications for HRM in the UK Armed Forces

ALEX ALEXANDROU
Cranfield University, Royal Military College of Science

INTRODUCTION

Since our last publication[1] there have been a number of significant developments in the area of HRM in the UK Armed Forces. These have taken the form of strategic Government initiatives and the publication of significant reports by the Ministry of Defence and the Defence Select Committee. The aim of this chapter is to outline the main elements of these developments and link them wherever possible to the subjects and themes being covered by the other contributors.

SPENDING REVIEW 2000

The Review[2] outlined the spending plans for all Government departments for the period 2001–02 to 2003–04, how the Government would allocate the funds, its criteria for improvements in public services and it set out a number of Public Service Agreements (PSAs). For the Armed Services, such an initiative will have a direct impact not only on their operational capabilities but also on the MoD's overarching HRM strategy.

On the surface the Review seemed quite favourable to the Forces. It argued that it provided real growth in the defence budget for the first time in over a decade by an average of 0.3% a year for the period 2001–2004. It would continue to ensure investment in new equipment for all the Services. Bring the Royal Navy and RAF up to full manning, try to achieve the same with the Army and tackle the issue of overstretch in the Armed Forces.[3]

The Review also set out four PSA targets for the MoD. Two of them it can be argued will have direct HRM implications. These are the ones that point to the need to:

- "Recruit, retain and motivate the personnel needed to meet the manning requirements of the Armed Forces, so that by March 2004, the Royal Navy and the Royal Air Force achieve full manning and the Army meets 97 per cent of its manning requirement".

- "Work with partners so that the European Union can, by 2003, deploy forces of up to Corps level (50–60,000 personnel) within 60 days, capable of undertaking the full range of Petersberg tasks in and around Europe."[4]

The new spending plan increases the MoD budget by £2 billion between 2000 and 2004. This is set out in Table 1 below.[5]

TABLE 1
DEFENCE SPENDING PLANS, 2001– 2004

	£ million			
	2000–01	2001–02	2002–03	2003–04
Total Budget	22, 975	23,570	24,198	24,978
of which:				
Resource Budget	17,750	18,076	18,485	18,731
Capital Budget	5,225	5,494	5,713	6,247

Once the figures are broken down, it is clear that from an HRM and particularly a manning perspective, the ideals of the Spending Review and the PSAs may be just that. A few hundred million pounds per annum spent on what can be termed strategic HRM issues such as recruitment and retention may not even be enough to maintain current levels let alone increase them significantly. In my view, in the greater scheme of things, such a small increase can be regarded as "paper clip" money and nothing else.

ARMED FORCES DISCIPLINE ACT 2000

Disciplinary issues within the Armed Forces are regulated by the three separate Service Discipline Acts (SDAs).[6] In effect this provides the three Services with their own legal systems, which in turn mirror as far as possible the civilian law system of the UK. In the past, these Acts have been renewed by the normal quinquennial Armed Forces Act, the most recent receiving Royal Assent in 1996[7] and this is still the case as evidenced by the presentation to Parliament of the Armed Forces Bill[8] in December 2000. However, it was felt that specific legislation was required before the new Armed Forces Act came into being because there was concern that the present SDAs may not comply with either the European Convention on Human Rights (ECHR)[9] or the recently introduced Human Rights Act[10] that incorporates a number of ECHR provisions into UK civilian law.

The new Discipline Act[11] thus ensures that on the issues of Summary Justice, Custody before Charge, Trial by Court-Martial and Summary Appeal Courts, the SDAs now conform with the ECHR. It is interesting to note that the Armed Forces Bill currently making its way through Parliament, carries a statement on its front page by the Secretary of State for Defence, Mr Hoon, that clearly indicates that in his view the provisions of the Bill are compatible with Convention rights.[12] The importance of the Human Rights Act[13] from an Armed Forces perspective will be discussed in greater detail in Chapter 2.

THE MINISTRY OF DEFENCE'S STRATEGIC VIEW OF HRM ISSUES

Whilst the Strategic Defence Review (SDR)[14] remains the driving force of the Government's overall defence policy, it can be fairly stated that it has become a little dated. To this end, the present administration has decided that the SDR needs to evolve and part of this evolution was unveiled earlier on this year with the publication of the strategic document entitled Defence Policy 2001.[15] This paper is a reappraisal of the SDR, which took account of the implications of recent events and emerging trends.[16]

Significantly from an HRM perspective, this strategic reappraisal not only examines current "people issues" but also clearly regards them as a central tenet of any defence policy. It argues that present and future capabilities depend on attracting, motivating and retaining sufficient quality people with the right skills.[17] It recognises that the MoD has to deal with the current changes in the demographic make-up of the workforce to ensure that the terms and conditions offered to the next generation of Armed Forces personnel are as attractive as those on offer in the private sector. To ensure that this is the case, the MoD states that it is adopting a comprehensive approach to its manning strategy to improve recruitment and retention. Among the immediate priorities (at the time of publication) were:

- Completing the upgrading of Service families accommodation

- Reducing disruption to home life suffered by Service personnel and their families

- Developing "family friendly" policies

- Completing the Defence Training Review

- Improving the terms and conditions of employment for civilian personnel.[18]

These are important strategic issues and will undoubtedly impact on the way the Armed Forces currently "do business". They will have implications for the culture and morale of current and future military personnel, issues that will be discussed from a number of perspectives in Chapters 3, 4 and 6.

INTRODUCTION OF A NEW PAY SYSTEM

In April 2001, the much vaunted and delayed new pay system for Armed Services personnel – Pay 2000 – was officially unveiled.[19] However, most of its contents were known in advance as will be explained below. It was supposed to have been introduced the previous year, hence its title but one can only assume that the mechanisms were not in place for it to go on-stream as planned.

The Armed Forces' Pay Review Body seems to have given the new pay scheme a cautious thumbs up. As it strongly indicates the new system will provide the flexibility to develop a closer match between pay and job weight, skills and experience. Interestingly the Review Body and the MoD

4

have worked closely to develop pay ranges for the new pay structures. The Review Body quite clearly regards the introduction of Pay 2000 as the first step in an evolutionary process, which will move on to ensure that such a system has a number of recruitment and retention aspects allied to it.[20]

The Pay Review Body has also stated that despite the new system coming on-line there are some outstanding issues. Most notably, it believes an appropriate development programme should be introduced as soon as possible if the new pay structure is to succeed, particularly with regard to recruitment and retention, which it views as critical over the next few years.[21]

An interesting aspect to the introduction of this new pay system is the input or lack of it from current Armed Forces personnel. Apart from the usual visits of the Pay Review Body, servicemen and women have had no real voice or input as to how this system has been developed and implemented, which is further evidenced by their inability to defend themselves when attacked by the media, politicians or even the public. For example, the Conservative MP Anne McIntosh recently claimed that there was a culture of political correctness and a tendency towards compensation claims in the Armed Services.[22] The lack of a collective voice or body to represent the views of Forces' personnel on these and many other topics is one of the issues that will be debated vigorously in Chapter 10.

DEFENCE COMMITTEE'S ANALYSIS OF THE SDR'S POLICY FOR PEOPLE

Throughout 2000, the Defence Committee examined HRM developments in the Armed Forces by focusing on what progress had been made with particular reference to the SDR's "Policy for People"[23] and the Armed Forces Overarching Personnel Strategy (AFOPS).[24] The examination focused not only on full-time military personnel[25] but also on the Reserves.[26]

In relation to full-time personnel, the Committee examined the issues of recruitment and retention, paying particular attention to ethnic minorities, women, manning problems and overstretch. It also sought to analyse how the Services should look after Service Personnels' families and the issue of post-service provision.[27] It is interesting to note that the Committee strongly believes that manning is the single most important element of the MoD's HRM strategy for the 21st century.[28]

Some of the Committee's findings make not only for interesting reading but also should be of some concern. These include the following:

- "Despite the healthy state of recruitment, it is clear that the manning problem is worsening rather than improving;

- The achievements of the Armed Forces in tackling the issue of racial discrimination are considerable – even if the actual results in terms of recruits remain a little disappointing, the culture change has, we believe, been profound;

- It is not clear, in enunciating this policy on women in combat roles, whether this exclusion is on grounds of physiological ability or moral distaste for women having to do such work. If it is the latter, it is time it was abandoned;

- We believe the Services have made great strides in changing their working environment to one where all members of society can expect to feel welcome. But there is no room for complacency: regrettable incidents of racial and sexual harassment and other forms of bullying are still occurring and efforts to eradicate these must continue;

- The recruiting agencies must assess whether appropriate safeguards are in place to guard against poor recruitment practices. They must also ensure that those selected to carry out recruiting are the most suitable people available, and that they receive the necessary training and retraining;

- It is extremely worrying that the target date for achieving full manning in the Army keeps receding;

- We cannot emphasise too strongly our belief that generous access to free communication with families is a fundamental right;

- The Armed Forces should do more to recognise and

accommodate the changing needs of personnel during their period of service. We recommend that the MoD takes a more imaginative approach to terms of employment in the Services and investigates in detail the possibility of offering career breaks and guaranteeing personnel with families more stability at periods in their career when they need it;

- A high standard of accommodation should be available to all Service families who want it. Achieving the upgrade of the estate in a reasonable time span is essential;

- We expect a comprehensive statement policy on unmarried partners in response to this Report and encourage our successor committee to give consideration to this important matter of principle at an early stage;

- We recommend that the MoD make resettlement training and advice an entitlement for Service personnel which should be available for up to 12 months after discharge;

- As we have commented before, the MoD has not in the past handled the issue of sick veterans with anything like the sympathy and concern it should demonstrate."[29]

Clearly food for thought, particularly from the perspective of recruitment and retention. These issues will be discussed in greater detail in Chapters 8 and 9, with a strong emphasis on the need for the Armed Forces to change their thinking, not only in terms of whom they target, but also what incentives they can offer both to entice people to join and also to stay.

The need to achieve this is ever more pressing as the latest UK Defence Statistics clearly show that there has been a further decrease in the overall number of Armed Forces military personnel from 208,600 in 1999 to 207,600 in 2000. When these figures are broken down by Service, the Royal Navy and RAF continue to show signs of decline while the Army registered a slight increase from 109,700 in 1999 to 110,100 in 2000.[30] However, as was clearly noted by the Defence Committee, this is unacceptable if the Armed Forces are to ensure that they can operate efficiently and effectively and deliver the quality of service that is expected of them.[31]

In relation to the Reserve Forces, the Defence Committee again not only unearthed some interesting issues but also showed that the Reserves too were experiencing difficulties in a number of areas. The Committee looked at three in particular, first, what it termed preparing the ground,[32] and then the restructuring and use of the Reserve Forces.[33] As the following table will show, the Committee noted that both the Naval and RAF Volunteer Reserve forces demonstrated a deficit in terms of trained strength.

TABLE 2
TRAINED STRENGTH AGAINST TRAINED REQUIREMENT – VOLUNTEER
RESERVE FORCES (DECEMBER 2000)[34]

	Trained Strength	Trained Requirement
Naval Service	2,574	3,887
Territorial Army	41,671	41,204
RAF	1,617	2,149

It went on to make a number of comments and proposals as to how the problems within the Reserve Forces could be dealt with. These included the following:

- "Greater use of part-time personnel, and greater flexibility of employment patterns, are features of the solutions sought by almost every civilian organisation facing personnel costs and/or skill shortages. Similarly, the government has frequently restated its commitment to forging a more effective alliance between the public and voluntary sectors. These are areas in which some radical thinking could be done by the Armed Forces."[35]

- "We hope that, in future, the MoD will be able to demonstrate convincingly that both individual training and unit training levels for the TA are being maintained at appropriate levels;

- It is time for the Reserve Forces fully to take up the task of supporting the Regular Forces' deployments of air forces abroad. Developing a proper career path for part-time Royal Auxiliary Air Force personnel and some formed flying units would be integral parts of this;

- The potential benefits to the NHS of generating more medical reservists should be more aggressively marketed by the MoD, now that more NHS senior management figures are on the Defence Medical Services Board;

- If failure to prosecute those who ignore their obligations as Regular Reservists is common knowledge both within MoD and the Reservist community it is obvious that the procedures are discredited. The MoD has to grasp the nettle and decide whether to enforce the current procedures – including prosecution – where necessary, or admit that current procedures have failed, in which case reform of the system, including legislation, should be made a high priority;

- The MoD needs to win the trust of employers if they are to release Reservists in the event of an emergency, and employers must be approached early in such situations for trust to be won and maintained;

- We expressed our doubt about the validity of the SDR calculation of the size of the TA, and noted at the time that events had often overturned previous defence reviews and shown how quickly and dramatically planning assumptions can be proved wrong."[36]

As the Committee quite rightly states, the last few years have been a turbulent time for the Reserve Forces.[37] It is with this in mind that we have attempted to take a different approach in examining the issue of military volunteers. The aim of Chapter 7 is not only to put forward new ideas as to how the Reserve Forces of the future should be made up but also to put some "meat on the bone" with regard to some of the Defence Committee's suggestions.

THE APPOINTMENT OF A NEW CHIEF OF THE DEFENCE STAFF

In February 2001, General Sir Charles Guthrie stood down as the Chief of the Defence Staff (CDS). However, in what can be termed as his valedictory speech[38] he managed to well and truly put the "cat amongst the pigeons", when he argued that the Services should not admit women to close combat roles if this damaged operational effectiveness. This was, to say the least premature, given that the MoD has not officially reported on the outcome of its investigation as to the validity of opening up more front-line combat roles to women.[39]

These comments along with a number of the issues already mentioned, notably recruitment and retention, are now being seriously considered by Guthrie's successor, Admiral Sir Michael Boyce. In evidence to the Defence Committee he alluded to some of his thoughts. On the issue of women in combat, the CDS did not rule it out and argued that if it did not affect capability then he saw no reason why women should not be on the front-line, as they are in ships and aircraft.[40] The contentious issue of women in the military will be examined from an interesting perspective in Chapter 5.

On the issue of undermanning, Boyce stated that the current position gave serious cause for concern and that the current level of accommodation was unsatisfactory.[41] With regard to the Reserve Forces, he was happy with where they were going in terms of restructuring and that they need to be a vital part of the UK's overall military capability.[42]

Admiral Boyce, on the evidence of his first few months in office, seems to have his "finger on the pulse" and may well prove to be a valuable asset to the Armed Forces. As Bruce George, the Chairman of the Defence Committee, has astutely noted, the new CDS has, uniquely, gained the endorsement of both *The Daily Telegraph* and *The Sun!*[43]

DEFENCE TRAINING REVIEW

Between September 1999 and April 2001, a comprehensive review of all aspects of military training was undertaken by the MoD. This resulted in the publication of the Defence Training Review[44] and as the Secretary of State for Defence, Geoff Hoon, quite rightly points out in the forward to the report, training is essential to the continuing operational success of the Services.[45] There were four key drivers that pushed for such a fundamental review and which were regarded as essential to underpin the need for change in Armed Forces training and education. These were the:

- Strategic Defence Review
- Shifting Social Trends

- The Challenge of Technology

- Wider Government Agenda.[46]

The conclusions and recommendations make for some interesting reading. I will not highlight all of them in this chapter but the following should give the reader a feel for where training and education is heading in the future. The report recommended:

- A progressive increase in opportunities for multinational training;

- Where there are common requirements, Service and civilian training should be integrated;

- To align with the MoD's specific operational support and business needs, a range of specialist modules such as business management and acquisition will be introduced into various officer training courses;

- The establishment of a small Defence Leadership Centre to design an overarching policy framework and strategies for managerial and leadership development;

- The MoD will seek progressive accreditation of all career educational and training provision;

- The creation of a Defence Undergraduate Bursary Scheme, with a number of civil universities providing the technical education required, which in turn would provide a more cost-effective means of training for all three Services;

- The creation of a Defence Academy to encompass the delivery of all postgraduate military education. It is envisaged that this Academy will become a centre of national and international excellence;

- Increase the amount of e-learning delivered with the proposal that 80% of appropriate classroom-based specialist training courses incorporate a minimum of 25% e-learning within five years;

- The need for cost-effective training and thus identifying areas of training that can be rationalised, particularly from a joint perspective;

- The establishment of a Director General of Training and Education to advance the MoD's goal of a more integrated, aligned, responsive and cost-effective education and training system.[47]

It is interesting to note that the report estimates that if all the measures it recommends are implemented there should be a net saving to the MoD in the region of £630 million.[48]

CONCLUDING REMARKS

As this introductory chapter clearly shows, there has been a plethora of initiatives and official reports that will significantly impact on the direction and success of the Armed Forces HRM strategy. They will have a direct influence on the culture and morale of present and future military personnel; the current recruitment and retention initiatives of the MoD and the three separate Services; the type of person that is not only being encouraged to join but who actually wants to join and whether they will be allowed to voice their concerns and opinions through a viable and officially recognised body.

Allied to the fact that member states of the European Union are discussing the creation of a European Army, which as Dempsey and Nicholl argue is taking shape faster then even its supporters may have dared to hope,[49] the issues and themes that will be addressed in the following chapters should not only add to the debate but enhance it in terms of a viable HRM strategy for the Armed Services in the future.

NOTES

1. Alex Alexandrou, Richard Bartle and Richard Holmes (eds.), *Human Resource Management in the British Armed Forces: Investing in the Future*, Frank Cass, London and Portland, OR: 2000.
2. HM Treasury, *Spending Review: New Public Spending Plans 2001–2004 – Prudent for a Purpose: Building Opportunity and Security for All*, Cm 4807, TSO, London: July 2000.
3. Ibid. p.65.
4. Ibid. p.66.
5. Ibid. p.67.
6. The Army Act 1955, The Air Force Act 1955 and the Naval Discipline Act 1957, HMSO, London.
7. Armed Forces Act 1996, HMSO, London.
8. Armed Forces Bill, TSO, London: 11 December 2000.
9. Defence Committee, *Session 1999–2000: Fourth Report, Armed Forces Discipline Bill*, TSO, London: 15 February 2000.
10. Human Rights Act 1998, TSO, London.

11. Armed Forces Discipline Act 2000, TSO, London.
12. Armed Forces Bill, op. cit.
13. Human Rights Act 1998, op. cit.
14. Ministry of Defence, *The Strategic Defence Review*, Cm 3999, HMSO, London: July 1998.
15. Ministry of Defence, *Defence Policy 2001*, Ministry of Defence, London.
16. Ibid. p.1.
17. Ibid. p.6
18. Ibid. pp.6–7.
19. Ministry of Defence, *Pay 2000*, Ministry of Defence, London: April 2001.
20. Armed Forces' Pay Review Body, *Thirtieth Report 2001*, Cm 4993, TSO, London: February 2001, paras. 1.16–1.17
21. Ibid. paras. 2.12–2.16.
22. House of Commons Hansard, *Debates for the 23 April 2001*, TSO, London: Col. 7.
23. Ministry of Defence, *The Strategic Defence Review and The Strategic Defence Review – Supporting Essays*, Cm 3999, TSO, London: July 1998.
24. Ministry of Defence, *Armed Forces Overarching Personnel Strategy*, MoD, London: February 2000.
25. Defence Committee, *Session 2000–01: Second Report, The Strategic Defence Review: Policy for People, Volumes I & II*, TSO, London: 14 February 2001.
26. Defence Committee, *Session 2000–01: Sixth Report, The Strategic Defence Review: The Reserve Forces*, TSO, London: 4 April 2001.
27. Defence Committee, *Session 2000–01: Second Report, The Strategic Defence Review: Policy for People*, op.cit.
28. Ibid. para. 2.
29. Ibid. paras. 23–170.
30. Ministry of Defence, *UK Defence Statistics 2000*, TSO, London: September 2000, p.39.
31. Defence Committee, *Session 2000–01: Second Report, The Strategic Defence Review: Policy for People*, op. cit.
32. Ibid.
33. Defence Committee, *Session 2000–01: Sixth Report, The Strategic Defence Review: The Reserve Forces*, op. cit.
34. Defence Committee, *Session 2000–01: Second Report, The Strategic Defence Review: Policy for People*, op. cit. para. 17.
35. Ibid. para. 18.
36. Defence Committee, *Session 2000–01: Sixth Report, The Strategic Defence Review: The Reserve Forces*, op. cit. paras. 9–48.
37. Ibid. para. 49.
38. General Sir Charles Guthrie, *Liddell Hart Lecture*, King's College, University of London: 12 February 2001.
39. Ministry of Defence, *Combat Effectiveness and Gender Study – 2000–2001*, unpublished to date.
40. Defence Select Committee, *Minutes of Evidence for Thursday 1 March 2001*, TSO, London: 1 March 2001, paras. 74–76.
41. Ibid. para.18.
42. Ibid. paras. 40–47.
43. Ibid. para. 101.
44. Ministry of Defence, *Modernising Defence Training*, MoD, London: April 2001.
45. Ibid. p.3.
46. Ibid. pp.6–7.
47. Ibid. pp.15–38.
48. Ibid. p.39.

49. Judy Dempsey, and Alexander Nicholl, "When push comes to shove", *The Financial Times*, Monday 30 April 2001, p.18.

2

You're in the Army Now!
Human Rights and the Armed Forces

ALLAN ROSS

Cranfield University, Royal Military College of Science

The traditional view that service in the Armed Forces in some way entails a limiting of personal freedoms and a temporary cessation of certain fundamental human rights has held sway without challenge since before the days of the Roman legions. The rationale for imposing such limitations on the Armed Forces is born out of the perceived necessity to impose a strict moral, social and ethical regime coupled to the requirements of discipline and obedience. This has been the nature of service in the Armed Forces throughout history. Even in the modern world such thinking still has a strong hold over the formulation of policy regarding the Armed Forces and service in them, and has to a large extent seen the Armed Forces falling into the second division vis-à-vis rights and their protection.

Beginning with 'Options for Change'; continuing with the ever increasing number of cases before the European Court of Human Rights (hereafter the ECHR); and culminating in the Human Rights Act 1998, there has been an obdurate movement toward the development of a new paradigm in human rights and their applicability to the Armed Forces. The last decade of the 20th century saw a radical shift in the perception of what service in the Armed Forces entailed or should entail, with a number of longstanding ideologies being successfully challenged before the courts. The Armed Forces now operate in an environment where women are no longer discharged on pregnancy, where women can serve in front-line units or on Naval vessels, and where the issue of homosexuality although no longer a bar to service is still a continuing issue which will require the MOD to clarify and strengthen its policy.

While few would argue that this has been a period of

considerable change for the Armed Forces the reality is that these developments, while significant, are merely the precursors of a radical change that will see the Armed Forces adopting HR strategies not out of place in commercial organisations. The truth being that the Armed Forces of the 21st century will be more akin to a commercial organisation than the traditional Army, Navy and Royal Air Force of the past. Officers at all levels will find themselves facing the dual task of adopting commercially aware policies whilst ensuring that there is no consequential 'impact on the efficiency or operational effectiveness of the service'.[1] Intrinsically linked with this will be the protection of the fundamental human rights of service personnel and the potential for conflict that this will bring about.

In October 2000 the Human Rights Act 1998 entered the statute books. The Act was seen by the Government as a representing a major shift in the protection of rights within the UK and formed the cornerstone of their legislative programme. A principle criticism of the protection of rights within the UK had always been that, first, the rights themselves were ill defined and often illusive; whilst second, their protection by virtue of their illusive nature was also ill defined and uncertain. The Human Rights Act was seen by the Government as redefining both the nature and scope of rights in the UK, while at the same time rectifying the long standing dichotomy between the UK and other European legal systems.

With the introduction of the Human Rights Act many observers predicted an explosion in litigation driven in part by an exercise of these 'new' rights granted by the European Convention on Human Rights (hereafter the Convention), and second by the prospect of large awards being made by the courts in respect of damages. This predicted increase in litigation has yet to materialise, and indeed will not materialise for three reasons.

First, the Judiciary has always considered that there exist adequate safeguards against human rights and civil liberty abuses within the UK, and on the whole this is the case.

Second, it would be erroneous to assume that the Human Rights Act incorporated the Convention into the UK legal order. The truth is that the Human Rights Act does little more than allow UK courts to monitor UK law to ensure it is compatible with the principles adhered to by the Convention. This in itself provides for a wholly different outcome than would have been the case if the UK had fully incorporated the Convention.

Full incorporation would have given the Convention direct effect within the UK thus allowing plaintiffs and defendants alike to plead each Convention Article directly, and that their rights under the Convention had been infringed. Although still able to make a plea that their rights under the Convention have been infringed, with the Human Rights Act falling short of direct incorporation it is for the judiciary to decide if a provision of UK law is broadly speaking compatible with the principle of the Convention. This in itself gives rise to a much weaker protection if for no other reason than it produces a much wider remit for claiming that UK law is in conformity with the Convention and therefore a wider remit within which to claim that there is no infringement of a person's rights.

The third reason why the Human Rights Act has not seen an explosion of litigation stems from the fact that the European Court of Human Rights (hereafter the ECHR) concerns itself only with judging alleged abuses falling within the various Convention Articles. The result is that the ECHR does not overly concern itself with the issue of damages and their quantum. The only award of 'damages' as such that the ECHR makes is based on criteria such as loss of earnings and legal costs. The English notion of 'damages' is therefore alien to the ECHR and the Convention. It is, therefore, well accepted that from a 'civilian' perspective there is unlikely to be a significant increase in litigation based on the Human Rights Act.

Unfortunately for the Armed Forces any increase in litigation is most likely to come from 'interest' groups seeking to bring test cases before the courts. These test cases will undoubtedly cover a myriad of issues, but the majority are likely to be based in areas where the issues are highly contentious and, at the same time, there exists a groundswell of opinion in favour of a developmental approach to the issue. In terms of what this means for the Armed Forces the future is far from settled, they will undoubtedly find themselves the centre of attention regarding test cases in areas such as sexual orientation, sex discrimination, and employment rights.

All these issues will have a part to play in moulding the Human Resource function of the Armed Forces in the 21st century. However, one issue stands alone in its implications for the Armed Forces, this being the current system of military justice and its almost total incompatibility with the ethos and principles of the Convention.

Service in the Armed Forces has always been viewed, at least by those in authority, as entailing some form of cessation of certain rights and a limiting of others. This view, although long founded, has increasingly come under attack in the latter part of the 20th and the early part of the 21st centuries. These attacks have come principally from members of the Armed Forces, and in particular from service personnel who themselves fall into minority groups. The reasoning behind this apparent high level of dissent among service personnel is manifold. However, even given this broad base it is possible to divine an underlying source. The Armed Forces have traditionally viewed themselves as being very much an homogenous body held together by common cause and purpose. This worked well while the MOD had no policies for dealing with issues such as racism, bullying, sexual harassment, and sexual orientation. In fact while all these issues were not only tolerated but also often condoned the Armed Forces presented a single homogenous front to the world.

This is not to say that these issues did not previously exist; undoubtedly they may have been less significant in their impact, although not because they were any less serious, but more likely because membership of a minority grouping was not something which the personnel involved would have wanted to highlight.

Ironically it may well be the introduction of the numerous zero-tolerance policies themselves that has acted as a catalyst for the increasing number of cases coming before the courts. Minority groups are no longer unsure about highlighting what they see as the inequalities of the system, while the backing they are now receiving from certain 'interest' groups is giving them the financial resources to state their case effectively.

It is the Human Rights Act that is the biggest change driver in the sphere of equality vis-à-vis military and civilian rights. Prior to October 1998 service personnel found a very limited forum within which they could focus public opinion. Indeed, a review of UK case law demonstrates an almost total absence of successful cases regarding service personnel when compared to the success of those cases taken before the ECHR. Even so the cost of taking a case to the ECHR, both in terms of time and the not insignificant financial burden, meant that few cases ever made it to the Court. Although it has already been stated that the Human Rights Act does little in the way of increasing the protection of rights in the UK this is only the case for the civilian population. The rationale for this is that the civilian population already enjoy a high degree of protection in all areas; the same cannot be said of service personnel who have often been denied the protection afforded to their civilian counterparts.

This denial of rights applies not only to past legislation but is still very much a part of future legislation. Even the European Union with its drive towards equal rights and opportunities has recently allowed Member States to opt out of allowing their Armed Forces the full protection of EU legislation. The Council recently promulgated *Council Directive 2000/78/EC Establishing a General Framework for Equal Treatment in Employment and Occupation*,[2] the purpose of which is to establish a European standard for the protection of employment rights. At Article 18 of the Directive the Council makes it clear that this Directive does not require, among others, the Armed Forces to recruit disabled persons. Many arguments can be proffered extolling the need to maintain a fit and able bodied military, however, the Article also makes it plain that there is also no requirement on the part of the Armed Forces to provide employment for those service personnel who are injured in the line of duty and whom cannot attain the required levels of fitness.

> "This Directive does not require, in particular, the Armed Forces and the police, prison or emergency services to recruit *or maintain in employment persons who do not have the required capacity to carry out the range of functions that they may be called upon to perform with regard*

> to the legitimate objective of preserving the operational
> capacity of those services."[3] (Emphasis added)

The Article, while allowing Member States to provide for the continuing operational efficiency of their Armed Forces falls into uncertainty by stating that such discrimination must be 'with regard to the legitimate objective of preserving the operational capacity of those services'.

What remains unclear is whether the Council is stating that such discrimination is legitimate *per se*, or whether such discrimination must be legitimate, and therefore subject to judicial scrutiny. If it is the latter interpretation that prevails there is unlikely to be a conflict with the Convention.

However, if the Council is attempting to circumvent the judicial process by declaring such discrimination to be legal the outcome is radically different. Both the Court of Justice of the European Communities and the ECHR have well developed case law regarding discrimination. Such an attempt on the part of the Council and the subsequent national implementation of such a measure would all attract the unrelenting condemnation of both Courts.

As stated the current system of military justice, both summary and Court Martial, is largely incompatible with the Convention and therefore a likely source of conflict vis-à-vis the Human Rights Act. While previously the only remedy available to service personnel was redress to the ECHR the introduction of the Human Rights Act circumvents this need and provides for the enforcement of rights at a national level. Although this is unlikely to see service personnel successfully pleading the provisions of the Convention before either summary hearings or Courts Martial it will still have a twofold effect.

First, service personnel will have a much more effective means of seeking a judicial remedy for infringement of their rights, and second, like the 'Service Test' contained in the 'Code of Conduct', local commanders will have to be much more aware of the rights of individuals when dispensing justice at all levels.

Military justice will undoubtedly have to develop a procedural system much more akin to 'civilian' law as the current system is seen by many as embodying the trinity of judge, jury, and executioner in two few fully independent bodies.

The case law of the ECHR has at times been scathing in its condemnation of military justice. Article 6(1) of the Convention states:

> "In determination... of any criminal charge against him, everyone is entitled to a fair and public hearing... by an independent and impartial tribunal established by law..."

In terms of the interpretation that is to be applied to Article 6 when concerned with military matters the ECHR has always considered that a general Court Martial, convened pursuant to the Army Act 1955, failed to meet the requirements of independence and impartiality set down in Article 6(1). The reasoning is based on the central role played by the convening officer. The ECHR holds the view that the convening officer is central to the applicant's prosecution and therefore too closely linked to the prosecuting authorities.

The role of the convening officer has been further condemned by the ECHR in as much as some members of the court martial may be subordinate (either directly or indirectly) to the convening officer, and further, that the convening officer is also the confirming officer. Such a centralised system of justice can never hope to satisfy the provisions of the Convention.

Even the amendments introduced by the Armed Forces Discipline Act 2000 are unlikely to satisfy the Convention as they do little to remove this intrinsic conflict of interests. Of course it must be noted that Article 6 applies only to criminal charges, however, the ECHR has as always taken a generalist view of the word 'criminal'. In deciding whether an offence falls inside the remit of Article 6 the ECHR will look at three criteria:

1. The classification of the offence by the law of the defendant state.

2. The nature of the offence.

3. The degree of severity of the possible punishment.

In civilian courts the classification of the offence, the first criteria, is relatively simple. On the whole a 'criminal' classification by the state will satisfy Article 6 in its entirety. Within the military such a distinct classification is unlikely to be available with many 'offences' being administrative in their nature. On this point the ECHR has relied heavily on the second and third criteria, and in the case of *Engel v. Netherlands*[4] the ECHR was called upon to decide what constituted 'criminal' vis-à-vis the Convention and the military. The ECHR took the view that military disciplinary proceedings can be dealt with by taking an autonomous meaning of the word criminal. In practice this means that matters concerning purely the internal regulation of the military are 'disciplinary' and therefore outside of Article 6; while 'offences' which carry penalties such as the deprivation of liberty are in essence 'criminal'. While giving some clarity such a restricted interpretation of the word 'criminal' fails to take into account all eventualities and as such lends itself to inequalities in the application of the Convention.

Mindful of this the ECHR has clarified this point and will now apply factors such as what is 'at stake' for the applicant.[5] Therefore, offences that lead to a dismissal from the service, a reduction in rank, or loss of seniority are likely to be caught by the provisions of Article 6.

In terms of the Convention and the current system of military justice further issues exist regarding Article 13 of the Convention, which states that :

> "Everyone whose rights and freedoms as set forth in this Convention are violated shall have an effective remedy before a national authority notwithstanding that the violation has been committed by persons acting in an official capacity."

The effective operation of Article 13 is essential to the cooperative relationship that must exist between the Convention and national legal systems. When read in conjunction with Article 26[6] this means that applicants must not only have access to an effective remedy but must also make use of these remedies. This relationship between Articles 13 and 26 places the primary responsibility for the protection of rights firmly on the state and national authorities. It must be stated at this juncture that Article 13 does not require an effective remedy for all possible kinds of illegality in the national legal order, rather it only provides for an effective remedy regarding rights protected by the Convention.

In terms of the military and its future relationship with the Convention, the Human Rights Act, and in particular Article 13, it is the requirement of 'institutional effectiveness' that is most likely to cause problems for the military judicial process. The ECHR has dealt with the issue of 'institutional effectiveness' by stating that it is only satisfied if the decision maker is 'sufficiently independent' of the authority responsible for the alleged violation of the Convention. In clarifying this further the ECHR has said that the fact that the official or body presiding is under the authority of the official or body responsible for the violation does not, in itself, render any remedy ineffective.[7] However, it would need to be demonstrated that the appeal authority in such a case did not merely endorse the decision without undertaking an independent investigation.[8]

In terms of the military, it is difficult to see how any of those involved in either the summary or court martial system could be held to be 'sufficiently independent'. This is so especially in light of the fact that the Courts-Martial Appeal Court has in the past been found to lack the necessary degree of independence within the disciplinary process.[9]

Even those changes brought about by the Armed Forces Discipline Act 2000, while welcome as a starting point, will in themselves fall short of the standards expected by the Convention.

In the last three years the military has been subjected to revolutionary, rather than evolutionary, forces all of which are driving the current changes in military Human Resource Management at an ever-increasing rate. As early as 1997 there were signs that the military was on a collision course with both the Convention and those changes affecting civilian HR management.

The current case law of the ECHR demonstrates first, that the military is not outside the influence of the ECHR, the Convention, and the Human Rights Act. Second, it acts as a guide, showing the future direction that both the military judicial and HR systems must take if the military and those that serve in it are not to remain in the second division vis-à-vis their civilian counterparts. Certainly with the military on a path that will place all non-operational jobs in the civilian sector it is inconceivable that the current inequities could prevail for much longer.

On the whole the military is currently in a period of remission regarding its HR and judicial systems and the Convention. The military should consider itself to be on notice that with the Human Rights Act attracting the attention of a number of 'interest groups' it can be only a matter of time before a fully funded challenge presents itself before the courts. With the Law Commission currently debating damages under the Human Rights Act it is conceivable that any future damages awarded against the MOD could be considerably in excess of those previously awarded by the ECHR.

NOTES

1. Code of Conduct.
    Http://www.mod.uk/policy/homosexuality/index.html
2. Official Journal of the European Communities. L303/16. 2.12.2000
3. Article 18. Council Directive 2000/78/EC Establishing a General Framework for Equal Treatment in Employment and Occupation. Official Journal of the European Communities. L303/16. 2.12.2000.
4. A22 (1976)
5. *Weber v. Switzerland* A177 (1980)
6. Article 26 of the Convention requires the exhaustion of national remedies before proceeding to the ECHR.
7. *Silver v. UK* A 61 at para. 116
8. *M and EF v. Switzerland* No. 12573/86
9. *Moore and Gordon v. UK* Application Nos. 00036529/97; 00037393/97

3

Military Culture Under Fire

HELEN WILDMAN
Adjutant General's Corps (ETS)

On 16 February 2001, the eve of his retirement as Chief of the Defence Staff, General Sir Charles Guthrie stated, 'The chiefs of staff must make it quite clear that, if they introduce women into the SAS or blind people into the Coldstream Guards, if they put social engineering and equal opportunities in front of combat effectiveness, there is a real danger of damaging something that really works very well.'[1] In the politically correct 21st century, military culture is under fire and General Guthrie was speaking for many, both within and outside the Services, who believe that the unique culture of the Armed Forces is being diluted to the detriment of operational effectiveness. Both the changes in attitude to the employment of women and the acceptance of homosexuals within the Armed Forces have had a significant effect on military culture, especially with regard to openness, masculinity, male domination and, some would argue, cohesion and efficiency.[2] This chapter will consider changes in military culture over the last ten years, with particular regard to the employment of women and homosexuals, in order to assess the effect on the operational effectiveness of the Armed Forces.

Christopher Dandeker believes that the Armed Forces have a unique culture. He states, 'The Armed Forces need to be different from other organisations because of the functional imperative that underpins all of their actions, namely warfighting.'[3] We therefore need to understand the make up of military culture in order to study how and, more importantly, why military culture has changed.

Culture has been defined as: 'The integrated pattern of human knowledge, belief and behaviour [that] consists of language, ideas, beliefs, customs, taboos, codes, institutions, tools, techniques, works of art, rituals, ceremonies...the development of culture depends upon man's capacity to

learn and to transmit knowledge to succeeding generations.'[4]
The majority of commentators define culture along these lines and include the concepts of beliefs, values, meanings and rituals. For example Deal and Kennedy define it as, 'A cohesion of values, myths, heroes and symbols'.[5] Although Dandeker may believe that military culture is unique, it still incorporates the same concepts as any other culture.

FIGURE 1
LEVELS OF CULTURE

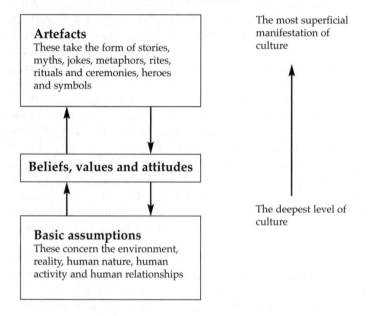

Source: Schein E. H. *Organisational Culture and Leadership*. Jossey-Bass, 1992.

One of the best known models of organisational culture is that of Schein (see Figure 1). Schein suggests that culture is best thought of as a set of psychological pre-dispositions (which he calls 'basic assumptions') that members of an organisation possess, and which leads them to think and act in certain ways.[6]
He identifies three levels of culture: artefacts, values, and basic assumptions. Artefacts are the things that one sees,

hears and feels when one looks at an organisation for the first time. In the Armed Forces they include such things as uniforms, badges of rank, parades, ceremonies, war heroes and regimental history.

Beliefs, values and attitudes are not quite so visible but they are still apparent, they are 'intimately connected with moral and ethical codes, and determine what people think ought to be done'.[7] In the military context this might include integrity, honesty, openness, belief in the cause, small group cohesion, regimental spirit, sacrifice and duty.

A basic assumption is very difficult to articulate as it is generally ingrained, unconscious behaviour. Brown suggests the following definition, 'a taken-for-granted solution to an identifiable problem'.[8] This can be best described as a deeply rooted behaviour shared by a group and which guides that group's perceptions, feelings and emotions. In the Armed Forces we would call this, 'military ethos'. As Gerald Frost states, 'The military ethos cannot be observed or felt directly, but can win wars.'[9] Schein's model is adapted at Figure 2 to reflect the military culture.

FIGURE 2
LEVELS OF MILITARY CULTURE

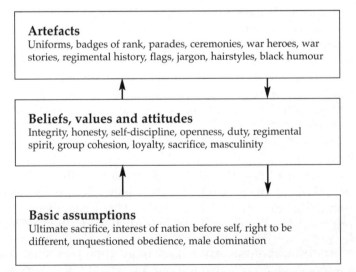

Artefacts
Uniforms, badges of rank, parades, ceremonies, war heroes, war stories, regimental history, flags, jargon, hairstyles, black humour

Beliefs, values and attitudes
Integrity, honesty, self-discipline, openness, duty, regimental spirit, group cohesion, loyalty, sacrifice, masculinity

Basic assumptions
Ultimate sacrifice, interest of nation before self, right to be different, unquestioned obedience, male domination

Adapted from: Schein E. H. *Organisational Culture and Leadership*. Jossey-Bass, 1992.

Change in the Armed Forces is an ever-present phenomenon. Over the last decade this has particularly applied to the 'basic assumptions' regarding women and homosexuals. In 2001, women are able to serve in 70% of trades in the Army, 73% in the Navy, and 96% in the RAF.[10] Women are now granted maternity leave as a right, paternity leave can be granted, single parents are accommodated in 'family quarters' (no longer 'married' quarters), homosexuality is legal, new Corps, such as the Adjutant General's Corps and the Royal Logistic Corps, are well established. Many older regiments and corps have disappeared, contractorisation is the norm and there is a positive equal opportunities policy.

Contrast today's military culture to that of 1990, just ten years ago, when women were forced to leave on pregnancy (married or not) employment of women was so restrictive that they wore a capbadge that spoke of their gender and not their profession,[11] homosexuals were dishonourably discharged and often imprisoned, and ethnic minorities were limited mainly to the Medical Services. There has been a huge cultural change in the Armed Forces in the last ten years, the two most significant cultural changes being the wider employment of women and the acceptance of homosexuals. These two changes will be considered in more depth.

Georgina Natzio believes that with the wider employment of women, 'military ethos itself was altered almost beyond recognition'.[12] Dandeker and Segal have identified four main factors that have led to the increase in the employment of women within the Armed Forces:[13] social, demographic and legal constraints; pressure from those women already in the Service for better career opportunities; advances in technology; and the attitudes of policy makers. These factors are significant when assessing why cultural change has taken place.

The expansion of military roles for women initially appeared to be spurred by the declining availability of eighteen-year-old males.[14] What has been called the 'demographic trough'. Between 1982 and 1994, the size of the 15–19 year old age group declined by 30%. This was a major concern for both military and civilian employers alike. The military launched its own internal inquiry into the problem[15] and the end result was the broadening of employment opportunities open to women. At the same time those women already employed by the Services were vociferous in their campaign to improve their career prospects.

Advances in technology meant that physical strength and aggression, embedded values in military culture, were becoming less important in a modern armed force.[16] Policy makers could not ignore this groundswell of opinion regarding the wider employment of women nor would the law allow them to do so. In 1976, a European Directive challenged the Armed Forces' exemption from the Sex Discrimination Act 1975.[17] It became apparent that, in law, exclusion of women from employments could only be justified on grounds of operational effectiveness, not traditional definition of gender roles.[18]

Tania Branigan believes that not much has changed since the demographic trough of the 1980s and that the move to recruit more women into the Armed Forces and to employ them more widely, is not just a matter of 'politically correct window dressing' but is still a necessity at a time when the Army has shortfall of soldiers of 8,000.[19] A recent MoD report states that by 2030 the number of people below the age of 20 is likely to fall by 900,000, and those aged between 20 and 40 by 1.8 million.[20]

The Armed Forces recruitment policy is being driven less by demands for equal opportunities than by a desperate shortage of personnel. Dr Rachel Woodward of the University of Newcastle believes that these recruitment problems have arisen

> "because the traditional pool of white, working-class northern males has dried up – or doesn't want to join up... The Army is at an absolutely crucial point. It's a huge institution built on many years of pretty strong ideas about gender identities, but all that is being challenged."[21]

However, there is evidence that the British Government is committed to continued gender integration not just because it is being forced to do so by demographic troughs, public opinion and the law, but for the added value that women bring to those expanded roles. This commitment can be gauged by the fact that in the downsizing of the Armed Forces in the post-Cold War context, the employment of women has not reduced as a result, as some might expect, but has continued to increase steadily.[22] Women currently make up 8% of the total Armed Forces, but 13% of recruits.[23]

Baroness Symons, the defence minister, has forecast that women will outnumber men in the military within 30 years. She also believes that there will be a woman Chief of the Defence Staff. 'within the foreseeable future'.[24] Her remarks were criticised as 'naïve' by senior officers who believe that to achieve a 50–50 split would imply that women would have to serve in substantial numbers – tens of thousands – in front-line fighting units and that even a much smaller number of women in front-line units would be detrimental to combat effectiveness.[25] Baroness Symons argues that this is not the case and that men should have any instincts to protect female colleagues drilled out of them so as not to impair their combat role.[26]

The Government's review of policy on homosexuality and the Armed Forces has given rise to equally heated views. The review followed a landmark judgement of the European Court of Human Rights on 27 September 1999, which deemed it illegal for an individual to be discharged from the Armed Forces on the grounds of homosexuality.[27] This ruling was swiftly followed by the issue of a 'Code of Social Conduct in the Armed Forces' introduced in January 2000[28] which lays down fundamental rules of conduct that apply to personnel regardless of sexual orientation. The Code recognises that,

> "The overriding imperative to sustain team cohesion and to maintain trust and loyalty between commanders and those they command imposes a need for standards of social behaviour which are more demanding than those required by society at large."[29]

The Code introduces a 'Service Test' which is to be used when considering possible cases of social misconduct. The test is, 'Have the actions or behaviour of an individual adversely impacted or are they likely to impact on the efficiency or operational effectiveness of the Service?'[30] The code has, in effect, lifted the ban on homosexuals in the Armed Forces.

It has been argued that cultural changes such as the wider

employment of women and homosexuals has taken place for demographic, technological and legal reasons. What is fairly clear from reading the literature is that the Armed Forces themselves were not the drivers for this change. For example, Gerald Frost believes that more than 80% of the Armed Forces were against the lifting of the ban on homosexuality.[31] The Government itself sounded less than enthusiastic about the move stating, 'There will be those who would have preferred to continue to exclude homosexuals, but the law is the law, we cannot pick and choose the decisions we implement.'[32]

Frost is quite clear that in his opinion, change has been forced on the Armed Forces not by the military themselves nor by the general public, but by pressure groups and minorities within a civilian society that is 'imposing its own socially egalitarian, hedonistic, litigious and risk-averse culture on the military way of life'.[33] He strongly believes that this is at considerable cost in terms of cohesion, and combat readiness.[34] He believes that these pressure groups are unable to comprehend that the values of an increasingly egalitarian society in which self-fulfilment and individual rights reign supreme and do not translate well to the military culture with its ethos of self-sacrifice and cohesion. In his opinion, military ethos, and therefore operational effectiveness, have been adversely affected as a result of this cultural change.

Frost is not the only commentator to believe that the imposition of the values of civilian society is damaging to the military culture as a whole. Kate O'Beirne quotes Professor Madeline Morris, a former consultant to the Secretary of the US Army, who believes that the military must rid itself of traits such as 'dominance, assertiveness, aggressiveness, independence, self-sufficiency, and willingness to take risks' in order for its gender integration problems to disappear.[35] These traits are the bedrock of military culture. Such dilution of the military culture would surely result in an Army that would be ineffective and suffer irreparable damage.

O'Beirne believes that there is compelling evidence that the presence of women in military units detracts from combat readiness, unit cohesion and military effectiveness. She states, 'With national security at stake, the need to maintain a strong military must take precedence over concerns about equal opportunity.'[36]

Such views are both widespread and international. The Israeli Army, often cited as a bastion of equal opportunities, does not allow women into its combat units in the infantry and tank corps as, 'there is a feeling amongst officers that, if these units were opened up to women, they will be devalued and men will not compete to get in'.[37]

Not all commentators are negative with regard to the wider deployment of women and the lifting of the ban on homosexuals. A recent study by the RAND Corporation concluded that gender integration becomes a minor issue if unit leadership is solid.[38] Duncan Lustig-Prean strongly advocates the move towards a Code of Conduct within the Armed Forces. He believes that as personnel are gelled into a team through military training, issues of gender and sexual orientation, which he classes as 'petty differences' dissolve. He states that:

> "It does seem to me rather extra-ordinary that Armed Forces who are capable of fighting so effectively 8000 miles away in the Falklands and in the Gulf and who can be relied on to project military power effectively in Bosnia, Rwanda, Kosovo, even Serbia, should be flummoxed by a minor personnel issue."[39]

To these commentators, while there is no evidence to suggest that Armed Forces necessarily thrive on changes to military culture, neither do they necessarily lead to a decline in effectiveness.

The Armed Forces are unique and they have a need to be different[40] but they would be foolhardy if they did not take note of the changing world in which they operate and adapt, to a certain extent, in order to reflect these changes. Certainly without some of the changes that have taken place over the last decade, they could not have survived: undermanning and overstretch would be far worse than current levels, retention would be worse and resources would have been wasted when highly trained female personnel and homosexuals would have been forced to leave. Compensation payments for both women and homosexuals would become untenable.

The military often resist change until ordered to do so by their political masters. Ade Ajadi believes that although cultural change in the Armed Forces may have been forced by legislation, 'the real benefits of sustainable commitment to equal opportunities and diversity will be immeasurable'.[41] However, enforced change is not a desirable attribute and does not make cultural change easily attainable. Dandeker warns that:

> "When you are trying to change the military culture of a first class fighting machine in a direction of which it is suspicious, you must balance the consequences of what you believe to be right and necessary on legal and moral grounds against the effects of moving on too quickly on, among other things, recruitment and retention. There are no easy and cost-free answers whichever decision is taken."[42]

British military culture has changed dramatically over the last decade. Change was necessary and reflected cultural changes in society as a whole. It is from this society, whose values change over the decades, that the Armed Forces recruit their personnel.[43] Today it is the 'basic assumptions' – Schein's 'deepest level of culture' – that are themselves being challenged.

The US Army has recently changed its recruiting slogan from 'Be all you can be' to 'An Army of One'. The campaign stresses individualism and is directed at what Louis Caldera, the US Secretary of the Army, calls the 'me-now' group. While recognising the importance of the basic assumptions of military ethos, Caldera states, 'You have got to get them in the door to try selfless service. And you've got to let them know that even though it is about selfless service, they are still individuals.'[44]

The key is to recognise that although the Armed Forces must change with the times, they are unique and that restructuring the Armed Forces in such a way as to make their practices and culture resemble that of contemporary civilian society does not come without costs. We must be wary of employing techniques that have proved to work in the civilian sector, on the Armed Forces or as Frost puts it, we must resist 'the imposition of a modern liberal vision on a society which is necessarily illiberal'.[45] The factors that make a factory or an office efficient may have the opposite effect if introduced in a warship or an airbase.[46]

Dandeker and Segal assert that 'culture is all about thriving and surviving'.[47] If this is so then the Armed Forces today are surviving. It could be argued that the wider employment of women thus far has enabled the Armed Forces to 'thrive' in a way that would not have been possible otherwise. However, many commentators believe that the sensible limits of the deployment of women have now been reached and that further expansion of the role would detract from combat effectiveness.[48]

The impact of the lifting of the ban on homosexuals in the Armed Forces has yet to be felt, although Ade Ajadi believes that 'the demonstrable progress made already, with regard to women and those from minority ethnic backgrounds, gives genuine cause for optimism'.[49]

At the other extreme some would argue that while some regiments have adopted an enlightened approach to the wider employment of women and the relaxation of the laws on homosexuality, there are others that remain, 'stubborn bastions of testosterone-charged intransigence'.[50] A balance must be found if the Armed Forces are to 'survive' and hopefully 'thrive'. This balance can be achieved so long as those imposing change upon our service-personnel recognise, and accept, that 'war is not an equal opportunities activity'.[51]

NOTES

1. Michael Smith, 'Guthrie Launches Final Assault on 'PC' Forces', *Daily Telegraph*, 16 February 2001
2. Frost, G. 'The Folly of Imposing a Liberal Vision on a Necessarily Illiberal Society', *RUSI Journal*, June 1999, p.95.
3. Dandeker, C. 'Don't Ask, Don't Tell, and Don't Pursue', *RUSI Journal*, June 1999, p.87.
4. *The New Encyclopaedia Britannica*, 15th Ed., Encyclopaedia Britannica Inc. (1992) Micropaedia, Vol. 3, p.784.
5. Deal, T.E. and Kennedy, A. A. *Corporate Cultures: The Rites and Rituals of Corporate Life*, (Penguin 1988) p.4.
6. Schein E. H. *Organisational Culture and Leadership* (Jossey-Bass 1992).
7. Brown, A. *Organisational Culture* (Pitman Publishing 1995) p.21.
8. Ibid. p.22.
9. Frost, G. *Not Fit To Fight. The cultural subversion of the Armed Forces in Britain and America*, (The Social Affairs Unit 1998) p.3.
10. Richard Norton-Taylor, 'New Forces Chief Accepts Women Could Die in Battle', *The Guardian*, 23 February 2001.
11. The Women's Royal Army Corps (WRAC) was founded in 1949 and disbanded in 1992. Between these dates all women, regardless of their professional qualifications, had to join the WRAC. WRAC officers could be

'permanently employed' with the Corps which related to their profession eg female engineers would be WRAC 'permanently employed' with the Royal Engineers. Male officers were able to join the corps of their choice.

12. Natzio, G. 'Homosexuality – Can the Armed Services Survive It?' *RUSI Journal* , December 1995, p.39.
13. Dandeker, C. and Segal, M. W. 'Gender Integration in the Armed Forces: Recent Policy Developments in the United Kingdom', *Armed Forces and Society*, vol. 23, no. 1, Fall 1996, p.37.
14. Ibid. p.39.
15. Ministry of Defence, *Manning and Recruitment in the Lean Years of the 1990s (MARILYN) – Report of the Adjutant General* (1989).
16. Dandeker and Segal, op. cit. p.37.
17. This was the Equal Treatment Directive of the European Commission, 76/207, 9 February 1976.
18. Dandeker and Segal, op. cit. p.39.
19. Tania Branigan, 'Sisters in Arms', *The Guardian*, 12 February 2001.
20. Michael Evans, 'Age Gap Problem Will Hit Recruitment', *The Times*, 8 February 2001.
21. Branigan, op. cit.
22. Dandeker and Segal, op. cit. p.31.
23. Branigan, op. cit.
24. Adam Nathan, 'Women "will dominate future army"', *The Sunday Times*, 14 January 2001.
25. Ibid.
26. Ibid.
27. Ajadi, Ade, 'Homosexuality and the Armed Forces', *Defence Management Journal*, Summer 2000, p.112.
28. Ministry of Defence *The Armed Forces Code of Social Conduct Policy Statement*, D/SP Pol 2/50/1 (January 2000).
29. Ibid.
30. Ibid.
31. Frost, op. cit. June 1999, p.96.
32. Ajadi, op. cit. p.112.
33. Frost, op. cit. June 1999, p.96.
34. Ibid.
35. O'Beirne, K. ' The War Machine As A Child Minder' in Frost, G. *Not Fit to Fight* (The Social Affairs Unit 1998) p.37.
36. Ibid. p.38.
37. Alan Philps, 'The Troops Who Take Their Guns On To The Dance Floor', *Daily Telegraph*, 22 January 2001.
38. Valpolini P., Sculte H. and Lewis, J. A. C. 'Gender and the Military – Women Warriors', *Jane's Defence Weekly*, 23 June 1999, p.25.
39. Lustig-Prean, D. 'Fit to Fight? – People are discharged for one private aspect of their private lives, not for any misconduct', *RUSI Journal*, June 1999, p.90.
40. Dandeker, June 1999, p.87.
41. Ajadi, op. cit. p.114.
42. Dandeker, op. cit. p.89.
43. Ibid. p.88.
44. James Bone, 'US Army aims for "me-now" generation', *The Times*, 11 January 2001.
45. Frost, June 1999, p.96.
46. Ibid. p.95.
47. Deal T. E. and Kennedy A. A. *The New Corporate Cultures* (Perseus Books 1999) p.35.

48. O'Beirne, op. cit. p.38.
49. Ajadi, op. cit. p.112.
50. Branigan, op. cit.
51. Frost, op. cit. June 1999, p.94.

How to Destroy an Army: The Cultural Subversion of Britain's Armed Forces

GERALD FROST

Almost all those who have had anything to do with the Armed Forces notice that they are different in a way that communicates itself immediately.[1] As with others in professions that claim a distinctive culture, professional servicemen differ from others by virtue of what they do. While adapting to a range of economic, technological and strategic changes many within the Armed Forces have so far been extraordinarily successful in preserving that difference, and with it a sense of their own identity. In this respect they are quite unlike those in other callings who have joined the dreary but familiar procession from vocation to profession, and from profession to trade.

At the core of that difference is an ethos which defines itself in action but about which members of the Armed Forces feel uncomfortable talking. In the words of a former British Army officer turned academic:

> "Ethos should be reserved for very special and infrequent usage for circumstances and events of the greatest significance...it could be what makes the British Army better than others. Yet for an army it can only have true validity when that character or genius is proved in operations or war and acknowledged by those outside the military. Used by the military of themselves it can come across merely as bluff bombast and bull. Ethos cannot be dictated, it can only be felt and observed indirectly. It is there. It can win wars."[2]

That ethos sustains a culture which has developed over time in response to practical needs, and whose special quality reflects the fact that members of the Armed Forces must expect to take lives and to risk their own. The distinguishing characteristics of military life – the emphasis on obedience, loyalty, honour, tradition, and self-sacrifice – all reflect experience of the attributes needed to perform their task.

Redefine the task and you change the culture; change the culture – or permit it to change under the impact of external pressures – and the ability of the Armed Forces may be impaired. The result is likely to be military who are confused about their role, and who come to display that most fashionable of contemporary ills: an identity crisis. Although the symptoms are much more advanced in some military units than others — and some, indeed, remain wholly immune to the contagion — it is evident that just such a process is underway.

Despite the signs of public complacency about the prospects for peace, it should be stressed that there is little public pressure for change. Distinguished service by British forces in the Gulf has reinforced the impression of dedicated and well-led Armed Forces capable of using force effectively and with discrimination. The public may not understand the requirements for operational effectiveness but there is no evidence of any kind to suggest that it is dissatisfied with the recent performance of the Armed Forces, or that it would approve of moves to change their fundamental character. In Britain polling data demonstrates consistently high levels of public regard for the Services. Among the general public few would wish to take issue with a former Chief of the Defence Staff who said that in 50 years the British Armed Forces had scarcely put a foot wrong.

Rather, the demands for change come from opinion-forming elites, from pressure groups, minority activists, and from cost-cutting governments enthusiastic to implement innovations that have led to greater efficiency in the private sector, but which cut across the grain of military culture. In the main, these seem reasonable and just because so familiar — after all, they have been applied in nearly every other walk of life. It is only when their practical consequences are exposed that it is possible to see how dangerous and destructive they actually are. The accomplices in this process of institutional subversion are those at the senior levels within the Armed Forces who for a variety reasons have failed to distinguish adequately between those reforms which are compatible with military culture and those which are bound to damage it, and those who know perfectly well what is at stake but have chosen to remain silent.

Although the pressure comes from a diverse range of sources, critics of the Armed Forces display two common characteristics.

The first is a high degree of indifference to the impact of their proposed measures on operational effectiveness whenever their proposals are met with practical objections.

The second is a belief that the values and mores which sustain the Armed Forces may be simply regarded as disposable relics that have lost whatever relevance they may have once possessed. In instances where these are thought to collide with those of modern liberal society it is taken for granted that it is the former which should give way. Both characteristics are displayed in the following passage from *The Financial Times* whose author predicted — wrongly as it turned out — that the Blair government would be tempted to allow the courts to take the 'tough choices' over whether to lift the ban on homosexuals:

> "...it seems too mean an attitude to an issue which is above all a declaration of principle. Rather than being dragged into change, it would surely be better to make a choice which says: "Yes, this will be deeply unpopular, and yes, it may damage our military effectiveness, but we are going to do it because it is right...Western society is not threatened by a monolithic enemy which demands the sacrifice of moral rights to experience...Its biggest challenge is to fulfil the promise of its own open and plural nature. It is time to show the grace and tolerance which all of the fighting was supposed to defend."[3]

This passage, typical in its way, demonstrates how poorly the culture of individual rights and self-fulfilment translates to a world which places great emphasis on community and self-sacrifice. It also brings home the selective nature of the tolerance which the author seeks to uphold since, quite obviously, this is not to be extended to the minority culture of the Armed Forces.

The respect for principle is equally selective: the principle of sexual equality which is the only principle the author believes relevant to a consideration of the issues. This, however, is a principle that collides with the traditional views about the obligations of the serviceman not to put personal interests above those of his unit; this, too, is a matter of principle.

Coming at the end of a century that has been the bloodiest in recorded history the most remarkable aspect of the passage quoted above, however, is the assertion that the damage done to operational efficiency as the result of lifting the ban on homosexuals is a strictly secondary issue, if indeed it matters at all.

A society in which the concepts of honour, authority, hierarchy and tradition play a decreasing role (and in which some of these are disparaged) may come to regard a culture which is defined in those terms as a permanent source of reproachment. It would seem that modern liberal society still feels the attraction of such virtues, even if it is incapable of finding a place for them. In the long run it cannot survive without them. The danger is not that the civil and military aspects of society have grown too far apart but that the military is failing to resist pressures to narrow the gap. For as Baroness Thatcher has pointed out, defence forces that met standards of political correctness would not merely be absurd; they would be a source of danger and instability.

The challenge to the military way of life might be less serious if advocates of PC were less universalist in their approach. Regrettably, they brook no exceptions or deviations from their norms, viewing the Armed Forces as new and exciting terrain on which to extend their campaign, seemingly oblivious to the fact that their own liberty and well-being are underwritten by a culture they seek to destroy. Nor do they show awareness of the possibility that society may he damaged in a less obvious way if the military no longer acts as an exemplar of virtues which may have a less prominent role among private citizens, but which are still widely admired.

It would be wrong to imply that all those at the Ministry of Defence are blind or indifferent to the consequences for operational efficiency of the changes urged upon them But the record of the past 25 years suggests that the general pattern is one of concession and of bowing to what is regarded as inevitable in order to stave off still worse outcomes. Unable to engage politically in order to defend themselves, the Armed Services now find that the number of those who can do so with authority on their behalf decreases year by year while their tormentors multiply.

More disturbing is the evidence that the reforms are having precisely the impact on cohesion and discipline that their opponents feared. The decision to integrate male and female personnel has led to a predictable increase in litigation, sexual harassment allegations and to consequent distractions; the privatisation of military back-up services and the 'sales chart' school of military efficiency have caused resentment and damaged morale. Over and above all this it would seem that the repeated use of military personnel for non-military purposes – as 'policemen in a global village' – has caused further confusion about the military vocation. All of this has coincided with a growing sense that the military leadership has not displayed courage in defending those whose silence and loyalty is taken for granted.

Among the most important of the factors which are transforming military culture has been the introduction – or reintroduction – of commercial ideas to military affairs which may be traced to the utilitarian thought of the eighteenth century. In fact military forces configured along commercial lines have displayed little courage and achieved little distinction on the field of battle; factors that make business enterprise efficient may have the opposite impact upon a regiment or warship.

In modern Britain the application of commercial ideas has led to the implementation of a range of management and cost-saving techniques, and to the privatisation of a wide range of activities previously undertaken by the Armed Forces themselves. The objection is not, however, to privatisation per se. There are instances where privatisation, for example of cleaning and laundry services, have achieved worthwhile savings without unduly disturbing the special character of the Armed Forces. The objection is to obtuse and unreflective schemes of privatisation without adequate regard for the consequences. The latter would certainly include the privatisation of the support services needed by expeditionary forces, which could be a violation of the time-honoured principle that such forces be self-sufficient.

Among functions that have been privatised are the servicing of aircraft, the training of RAF pilots, the provision of engineering support, the management of non-military stores, and the repair of much army equipment. The intrusion of so many civilians dilutes the unique flavour of the military setting, disturbing the system of hierarchy upon which order and discipline rest. It also strikes at the systems of internal support which sustain Service families in times of crisis.

This truth was grasped by Baroness Park, a wartime member of the Special Operations Executive, in condemning a scheme that has aroused more anxiety and anger than any other privatisation measure – the decision to sell the entire married quarters estate – around 60,000 houses and flats – to a Japanese-led consortium on a lease-back basis. She told the House of Lords:

> "When two Welsh fusiliers were taken hostage in Bosnia some years ago, the press rushed to see the young wives, demanding to know what counselling they and their children were receiving. They were told proudly that the regiment and the regimental wives did that. They knew the score. That is what the regimental 'patch' is. Those who live there now feel threatened ... Widespread loss of morale and widespread anxiety ... is a high price to pay."[4]

Although subsequently modified, the scheme – like so many other schemes to save the Armed Forces money – does not seem to have been an economic success: it has been severely criticised by the House of Commons Public Accounts Committee. Privatisation has gone further since Antony Beevor wrote his authoritative account of life inside the British Army, but his account of attitudes towards privatisation still holds good:

> "Some cases have worked well ... Others have led to a disastrous decline in quality and reliability, mainly because of the high turnover of staff in the contracting companies ... The impression of a blanket policy to save money has caused great resentment."[5]

Along with privatisation has gone the introduction of management techniques to an area where 'productivity' is often impossible to measure, and where statistics may do more to obscure the truth than to reveal it. In this respect successive British governments seem to have learned little from the reforms of Robert McNamara which received their ultimate test in Vietnam. Martin van Creveld wrote of General Westmoreland's military administration there:

> "The men who designed the system and tried to run it were as bright a group of managers as has been produced by the defence establishment of any country at any time, yet their attempts to achieve cost effectiveness led to one of the least cost-effective wars known to history."[6]

It is not the immediate impact of such measures on cost or efficiency which should most concern us but the gradual replacement of military culture with that of commerce. The ultimate step in this process will be that the protection of the citizen – the first duty of government – will be contracted out. At that stage the moral content of the soldier's duty will have dissolved and war been subverted as a moral activity.

The final irony will be that measures introduced in the name of efficiency will leave the Armed Forces far less able to fulfil their purpose than before. For the loyalty of the mercenary is a tradable commodity and unlike the professional soldier who has heeded the call to arms, all of his calculations are based on his desire for longevity and the opportunity to spend the spoils of war.

If commercialisation diminishes the moral significance of a decision to serve the Armed Forces of one's country, and thus influences the character of the recruit, so too does the deployment of women at or near the front line. Young men have always been attracted by the martial ethos and the opportunity to prove themselves in battle. It is one way to win the respect of other men and the admiration of women. But in order that women can have successful 'careers' within the Armed Forces the tasks which men do better than women have to he played down, thereby diminishing the male's sense of accomplishment and process of exclusivity ('male bonding') upon which the cohesion of any fighting unit depends.

As in the United States the proper role of women is the most consequential as well as controversial issue confronting the British and US Armed Forces, one which will not be resolved until agreement is reached about the role of the Armed Forces themselves. If their first obligation is as an equal opportunities employer, then any reform to achieve gender integration can be justified; if, on the other hand, their purpose is the traditional one of fighting and winning wars, then no innovation which impairs that ability should be contemplated. It is evident that no lasting or mutually satisfactory compromise can be struck between these two positions; it also evident that in the US, as in Britain, it is the first of these propositions that is gaining ground.

War and the preparation for it, it needs to be remembered, are not equal opportunities activities. Even in the age of the cyber warrior and the high-tech warrior they are activities which still favour the quick and the strong. Women are not as quick or as strong. Women are not as physically strong: an average 30-year-old has the aerobic capacity of a 50-year-old man and is far more likely to injure herself during exercise. Women possess not much more than half of the male's upper-body strength, and only 72 per cent of the male's lower body strength. On average they run less fast, and can perform fewer sit-ups and push-ups. Women are more likely to be sick, perhaps as the result of pregnancy, and a higher proportion are single custodial parents (with the result that the US Armed Forces are now the biggest provider of child care in America).

Making sure that women pass the same tests of physical stamina as men will limit the number of women able to join, and also ensure that female recruits are of greater physical strength than otherwise might be the case. But experience in other countries suggests that the services will come under considerable pressure to introduce easier tests or to adopt 'gender-normed' testing. So many concessions to the forces of political correctness have recently been made that those in the vanguard of change have every reason to hope for further success.

Yet even if the line is held, this will not solve other problems. These include those that arise from placing young men and women in their prime of life in close proximity to one another on board ship or in tanks. The integration of women into the services has already resulted in some unfortunate court cases and unwelcome publicity, a great deal of distraction from the proper task as well as a good deal of unease among service wives. To open up additional roles to female recruits seems likely to reduce unit cohesion, impair morale and increasingly turn service officers into marriage guidance counsellors.

An American journalist and broadcaster, Kate O'Beirne, who served in President Reagan's Commission on the Assignment of Women in the Armed Forces, has put matters well:

> "The cultural liberalism that views training to kill the enemy as mere extension of working outside the home is in conflict with military realism. The problems of gender integration arise from the fact that men and women are different and in the unique world of the military those differences matter."[7]

Over and above the factors described there is evidence of a pervasive sense that senior officers in a position to discourage such trends have not done so with the courage and resolution expected from those they command. Outspoken criticism of what is occurring is actively discouraged or punished. In the US criticism of the moves to further integrate female personnel has been construed as sexual harassment. In Britain the Armed Forces are forbidden to take a view about the likely commitment of a mother in war, and when a senior British general held up the Canadian Armed Forces as an example of defence forces that have actually been rendered unfit for war, he was forced to retract and apologise.

Part of the difficulty lies in the understandable reluctance of senior officers to frustrate the wishes of democratically-elected governments. This is a predicament which is shared by others in the public service, but in most cases those affected are able to contribute directly to debate, thus ensuring that far-reaching policy changes are informed as well as democratically sanctioned.

In probing the reasons why senior US officers have not been more outspoken themselves, John Hillen, a former officer in the US Marines, has reached a gloomy conclusion; it is that with a few notable exceptions senior officers have effectively exchanged the identity of their service in return for short-term accommodation with anti-military elites.[8] Having ceded the terms of the debate to their enemies they are now prepared to sacrifice its ethics and culture, and if necessary to conceal the consequences. In short, they have failed to resist the imposition of a modern liberal vision upon a culture which is necessarily illiberal, and which is now disintegrating under the impact.

Serving officers in the UK Armed Forces presently contemplating a series of changes whose purpose and rationale they find inexplicable have ample reason to reflect on how far this interpretation explains their own experience.

Such accusations are more likely to be aired publicly in the US where the debate about the impact of PC on military culture has aroused wider interest than in the UK. There can be no doubt, however, that there is wide resentment at the failure of the Whitehall warriors to raise their heads above the parapet in order to fight off unwelcome changes. One notable exception was that of the First Sea Lord, Admiral Sir Jock Slater, who publicly echoed the warnings of General Colin Powell in the US in urging that the ban on homosexuals should remain. No other senior officer spoke out in support of Slater. Nevertheless his stand was instrumental in forcing the then government to hold the line.

Slater had also voiced reservations about the controversial sale and lease back of the married quarters estate referred to above. At the time he was regarded as a clear favourite to become Chief of the Defence Staff, not least because there had been five soldiers and airmen in a row, but he did not receive the expected preferment. Within the forces there is a widespread belief that his courage and his loyalty to the best interests of his Service, as he saw them, effectively disqualified him from the job.

It is clear that those anxious to somehow preserve the special feature of military culture cannot expect a sympathetic appreciation of the problem by parliamentarians. Ignorance about the realities of service life among MPs, lawyers and civil servants has grown as the survivors of the Second World War and the majority of the National Service generation have retired or died.

One consequence has been the application of civil law to the military sphere. Despite the shrinkage of the Services this resulted in a sevenfold increase in negligence claims against the MoD,[9] between the years 1991 and 1996 and a steady rise since that time. This explosion in litigation is undermining leadership through the discouragement of risk taking. It is also having the effect of promoting individual over collective interests – thereby reversing much of what the recruit absorbs in training – and of weakening the bonds of comradeship.

Yet another example of the values and practice of an increasingly risk-averse civilian society being imposed on the armed services has been provided by the bizarre decision to apply unadapted health and safety legislation to the Services and to training for what, after all, must be among the least healthy and safe of human occupations; this is producing obvious absurdities, while absorbing scarce resources. For example, lifts have now installed in military buildings for the benefit of disabled civilians when most users are those whose robust physical health is a condition of service.

Officers and non-commissioned officers must now take time off from military tasks in order to train for a variety of responsibilities governing fire, environmental, health, safety in the workplace and a range of other matters. Officers may well have to call off a mission or training exercise for fear of breaching civilian drivers' legislation even in theatres such as Bosnia. If an accident follows a decision to ignore the rules an officer could face a severe reprimand, but if he sticks consistently to them, his goal may have to be abandoned or training standards jeopardised.

The indifference of those in the vanguard of political correctness to arguments of the kind listed above suggests that they are at war not merely with what they see as prejudice, but with human nature itself. For theirs is a world in which soldiers, airmen and sailors are so amply blessed by nature that they can be expected to excel in the gentler virtues of sensitivity and thoughtfulness as well as the vigorous virtues of courage, honour, and audacity; in which homosexuals are consequently able to form relations with their fellows without fracturing the cohesion of the unit; in which women soldiers can perform the same physical feats as men; in which young males and females work in cramped physical conditions but do not form attachments that give rise to conflict, or exploitation or distract from the task at hand. It is, in short, an impossible world, one from which war and even the prospect of war has been conveniently banished.

NOTES

1.   This essay is based on the author's Introduction to *Not Fit to Fight: The Cultural Subversion of the Armed Services in Britain and America* (Social Affairs Unit. London, 1999).
2.   Mileham, Patrick, *Ethos: British Army Officership 1962–92*, Strategic and Combat Studies Institute, issue no.19.
3.   Gray, Bernard, *The Financial Times*, 3 May 1997.
4.   House of Lords, *Hansard*, 11 July 1996.
5.   Beevor, Antony, *Inside the British Army* (London, Chatto and Windus, 1990) p.472.
6.   Van Creveld, Martin, *Command in War* (Cambridge, Harvard University Press, 1985) p.260.
7.   O'Beirne, Kate, 'The War Machine as Child Minder' in Frost G. (ed.) *Not Fit to Fight*, op. cit.
8.   Hillen, John. 'The rise of the political general and the loss of the military identity.' in Frost G. (ed.) *Not Fit to Fight*, op. cit.
9.   Brazier, Julian, 'Who will defend the defenders?' in Frost G. (ed.) *Not Fit to Fight*, op. cit.

5

Women in the Military: Future Prospects and Ways Ahead

Caroline Kennedy-Pipe
Department of Politics, University of Sheffield

Stephen Welch
Department of Politics, University of Durham

INTRODUCTION

Some parts of feminist discourse on war and peace have for a number of years been preoccupied by the relationship which exist between women and national militaries. Armed forces have appeared throughout feminist writing in a number of guises, often as a powerful symbol of patriarchy and domination. While much of the feminist theorising about women and war has been tied into a specifically American context, some of these ideas, most obviously those associated with what we might term 'Liberal feminism' have informed debate within the United Kingdom. Specifically, we have seen the demand, based on ideas of sexual equality, that women be permitted to serve in all aspects of the Armed Forces and that there be an equal representation of women within the ranks and the command of the services.

Important though these debates have been, as we go on to argue, much of what has been the traditional liberal feminist critique of the military is really no longer relevant to the context in which the role of female servicewomen is discussed. Why is this? The first reason is that the goal of what we may describe as Liberal feminism is to some extent in the process of being achieved: women are now in the United Kingdom included in increasing numbers in military structures and attain higher levels of office. This is partly as the chapter will go on to argue because the Revolution in

49

Military Affairs (RMA) makes the issue of female 'effectiveness' in war less relevant but it is also the result of changes in society's expectations which make gender exclusion less sustainable. Indeed perhaps the crux of the second half of the chapter is that the inclusion of women in militaries in Liberal Democratic societies is crucial because the exclusion of such a group means that the military establishment is out of step with the way in which democracies conceive of themselves and the norms which govern such societies.

This is especially important because of the tasks which national militaries are now expected to engage in. With the transformation of mission in most Western militaries including that of the British services away from the exclusive provision of national security to engagement in the business of humanitarian intervention or in Peace Support Operations (PSO) the 'legitimacy' of those who intervene is increasingly important.

WOMEN, MILITARIES AND MILITARISM

Part at least of the broad feminist agenda has been to achieve parity of treatment between women and men, and the method has been the simple one of eliminating barriers to entry by women.[1] The military is one of the central institutions of the state, and is thus *ipso facto* a repository of political power and prestige. Like other central institutions, such as the representative and judicial institutions, it has historically been under the control of men. It is thus, like them, a bastion of political patriarchy, and like them, it needs to be changed. The demand is to undo the framework of political subordination of women by gaining entry, a solution simple in principle though of course historically very difficult to achieve in practice. The military retains key significance because of its somewhat more prolonged resistance to efforts to equalise access.

The military has symbolic and political importance for a large number of states and their populations. Feminist critics have addressed this in terms of patriarchal discourse, which will be discussed shortly, but they have also pointed to practical demonstrations of it such as the recruitment relationship between military and political elites. According to Jill Steans, experience in combat can still, even in the contemporary era, be a way of earning high office, or in a country such as the United States, a way of securing political election.[2]

Just as ancient civilisations gave special respect to citizens who had proved themselves in war, it can still be a special mark of respect to be a war veteran. This is an honour, Steans argues, which overall is denied to women. Women have traditionally been thought unfit or unsuited for the holding of high offices associated with the military or issues of national security. If women were rarely recognised as warriors, they are still equally unlikely to be head of the Royal Navy or the Royal Air Force.[3]

The direct political advantages accruing to men as a result of successful military service (Steans also alludes to economic benefits in the US such as free health care and cheap loans)[4] are not, in the view of critics, the only contribution made by the gender characteristics of the military to the overall pattern of female subordination. Indeed, much more often stressed, in keeping with the change in focus of what can be termed second-wave feminism, is the cultural aspect of subordination. Women's partial exclusion from the military and in particular from combat roles is held to exclude them from an important sphere of value, and thus to derogate them.

The values of honour and heroism are two components of this 'value' sphere. Military service for one's country has been regarded as an honour. War was, and many would argue still is, associated with masculine values such as physical strength, honour and courage. It is quite clear that there is a close connection between masculinity and warfare, in both historical-practical and discursive terms. In certain societies, those men that would not or could not fight might have been classified as 'women': some were even been made to don dresses as a sign of their weakness.[5]

Norman Dixon, for example, has argued that various British military conventions were designed to subordinate characteristics or habits regarded as female: so piano playing and art were denounced, long hair regarded as 'womanly', hence the regulation 'short, back and sides' and 'defensive' assignments such as convoy duty regarded as really rather shameful tasks.[6]

This misogynistic aspect of military practice finds an extreme yet common expression not just in 'boot camp' training but in the paradoxical treatment of women as either the 'spoils of war' or the 'protected'.[7] In the former category the rape of women during and after conflict is now well documented,[8] as are instances of the use of rape as a 'tactic' of war to humiliate or demoralise the enemy. We have many examples from the mythical raping of the Sabine women to the mass rapes witnessed in the recent Balkan Wars of how women may be used in war.[9]

Alongside such blatantly oppressive discourse and practice runs a quite different but, in Steans's view, complementary discourse and practice: that of protection of women by the military. Women in warfare have been regarded as defenders of the 'home front', an expression in wartime of their customary domestic duties.[10] Moreover, the vulnerability of the family and its female custodians provides a significant motive for participation in military conflict. Both culturally and in institutional terms, the function of 'protection' has been linked to masculinity. The phrase 'women and children' is one commonly used to symbolise the place of the female within the community. For this reason, women continue to be second-class citizens dependent on men for protection. Steans argues that such associations of masculinity – strength and femininity – protected have been necessary for the very conduct of war.[11] Part of the rationale for many men in war was to 'protect women and children and the rest of the familiar world back home'.[12] This argument also links to the debates about the psychological effect that women in combat might have on the morale of their fellow and male comrades.[13] A debate to which we will return.

From the gendered character of values of honour and heroism that are expressed by military narratives, critics make still broader claims as to the masculinity of discourses of citizenship, security and the state itself. The relationship between the bearing of arms and citizenship has a long history in Western political thought. Judith Hicks Stiehm, for example, argues that we in the West have traditionally held militarised conceptions of citizenship and that different categories of citizenship arise from the classes of those excluded from military service. The very young, the old, the disabled and, in some societies, the homosexual are barred from combat. Within this rubric, women are excluded, along with the infirm, from a full and equal role in military establishments. Women are also, according to this line of argument, effectively marginalised and disengaged from the business of defining, or redefining the 'national interest' and decisions as to when state sponsored violence should be/could be used to achieve them.[14]

Undoubtedly the claims made by some feminists as to the gendered discourses of war fighting and civilian–military relations can be contested. The association of military service with heroism and ensuing social and cultural prestige certainly finds a counter-example in the case of returnees from the Vietnam War, who might find it difficult to recognise their treatment after war as that of heroes or to agree that their combat experiences advanced them socially.[15]

It is also questionable whether exemption from the obligation to participate directly in fighting and risk death is quite so obviously as Steans claims a case of second-class status. It is, after all, an exemption shared by those holding the highest statuses in the Armed Forces. (Women have of course occasionally been military heroes, one could think for example of Joan of Arc, or indeed, Boadicea. Contemporary scholarship has also uncovered numerous examples where women have not only supported the role of men in war but participated in civil war and war itself.[16])

Nevertheless, it would be hard to argue against the general thrust of these feminist arguments, which can be summarized in Jean Bethke Elshtain's assertion that a distinction between 'beautiful souls' (women) and 'just warriors' (men) has been at the heart of most contemporary theorising about the respective role of women and men in both war and society.[17] The military is typically, thanks to its role in the birth and consolidation of most states, a central institution of the state, both functionally and symbolically; it is a male institution which is a key repository of classically masculine values, expressed both in the training given to its personnel and in the regard in which its greatest achievers are held; and women are placed in a relation of dependency upon it, as well as vulnerability to it, by virtue of their symbolic association with civilian duties as well as their partial formal exclusion.

However, these Feminist arguments about the relationship between military and society display a number of tensions, of which the most obvious is that between a separatist and potentially essentialist feminist anti-militarism and the view that the military represents an institution or a value sphere that women need to take over in order to achieve equality in society. The possibility should be considered, however, that the debate as a whole, and therefore this tension too, has been superseded by developments in the use and nature of military forces.

The next part will discuss two sets of developments which might seem to offer an eventual resolution of the conflicts outlined in this part: developments in technology, and in the missions of the Armed Forces of democracy. It will discuss the extent to which the former diminishes the force of certain traditional objections to the full incorporation of women in militaries, before considering whether current and future military assignments are themselves eroding the civilian–military distinction.

TECHNOLOGY AND MISSIONS

In post-industrial societies, certainly one such as the United Kingdom, the military does not occupy a central role. This is, in part because the relationship between the state and war has evolved. National militaries are shrinking, many societies are moving away from conscription and 'militarism' is no longer the force it was. Since 1945 there has been gradual erosion of the state's military demands on its peoples: a trend accelerated by the decline of Communism. By 1991, when the Soviet Union ceased to exist, Britain was relying on relatively small volunteer forces. France too has announced that it will abolish conscription within the coming decade. In some democracies, the notion of citizen as soldier has withered.

Many democracies, including the United Kingdom are simply unable to attract large numbers of young men into service life. There is, in the words of Christopher Dandeker, a 'demographic trough' in terms of the declining availability of eighteen-year-old males.[18] Nowadays, indeed, it is necessary to employ a range of tactics to find young men. While in some parts of the developing world, male children might be kidnapped to join paramilitary or national armies, in other states professional recruitment agencies are used in order to find young people willing to join the Army. In Scotland, for example, the Army has employed just such agencies in a bid to promote itself as a modern career option.

As this process of the decentring of the military has occurred, in some countries at least, there has been a corresponding reduction in the scope of exclusions of women. There is little that is new in women 'filling' in for an absence of men in the armed services. The experiences of women in war historically point to greater recruitment of females at times when men were in short supply and indeed, as Cynthia Enloe has argued,[19] a far greater female participation in combat roles if the preferred pool of male labour dried up. But there is now in the post-Cold War world an additional dynamic at work. After the end of the Cold War, the mothballing of airbases, the closure of nuclear bases and the eradication of intermediate-range nuclear forces are all visible symbols of the removal of the military from society and perhaps the centrality of the military to the lives of the young. Hence declining applications from young men and a corresponding need to attract women into parts of the Armed Services.[20]

This has certainly been so in the case of the British Army. Christopher Dandeker has pointed out that in 1991 (the year of the final Soviet collapse) considerable changes had taken place in the way that women were treated in the forces. For example, 100 of the 134 trades in the Army were open to women and the army had developed a policy of 'gender free' physical testing so that physical aptitude as opposed to sex would determine specialisation. In the same period, field training became part of the overall training schedule for women and they were allowed up to eight kilometres from the front line. During the Gulf War, 1110 British women served in various capacities, representing the first deployment of female personnel during war since World War II.[21] According to the House of Commons, Defence Committee, by the end of the twentieth century, women were serving in 70% of posts in the Army, 73% of posts in the Navy and 96% of posts in the RAF. However, women accounted for only 8.8% of officer ranks in the Army and 7.8% of other ranks.[22]

It is an interesting question whether the progress made in reducing exclusions is a measure of the success of feminist 'parity of treatment' arguments (underpinned by employment legislation both within the UK such as the Sex Discrimination Act of 1975 and through legislation enacted by the European Community) perhaps simply as a generalisation of achievements elsewhere (maybe the old assumptions regarding mental and physical capacities have finally reached the stage of exhaustion), or whether in fact it is precisely the reduced salience in institutional and value terms of militaries that have made this increased entry possible. However, for those who have traditionally opposed the masculine discourse of militarism, such a decentring of militarism is to be welcomed.

It is also the case of course that women have gained greater access to the services as the nature of warfare, certainly as experienced by those in countries such as the United Kingdom, has evolved. Even if we do not yet live in a post-heroic culture, as Edward Luttwak has claimed, war in the sense of trial by national survival is almost certainly dead.[23] We, or those in the West European world, live in an environment where war is at a distance, casualties are minimised and the preferred option of democratic states at war appears to be that of aerial bombardment. Such wars seem to have little to do with what traditionally would have been recognised as the reality of national wars. Thus, Baudrillard felt able to formulate his polemical claim that 'the Gulf War did not take place'.[24] Wars at a distance have changed the way in which modern militaries fight and the way in which civilian populations respond.

So, for example, the Kosovo campaign was conducted by the Western alliance without a single combat fatality. This is not the same as arguing that war is now casualty-free or any less destructive: for those on the receiving end of 'virtual' war, the opposite is probably true. Yet, this mode of warfare changes the role, and hence the nature, of soldiers or warriors. Christopher Bellamy, in his work *Knights in White Armour*, asked the question what type of 'future warriors' we might need. His answer was that for the new art of 'war and peace' 'we', presumably those of us in democratic states, will need soldiers capable of the following range of tasks:

> "to act as an ambassador, the lone representative of his or her country, or the UN at a disputed barricade. To carry sacred artefacts from a church for safekeeping. To operate night vision equipment, laser rangefinders and the 'battlenet' – a battlefield computer system similar to that in use in most big city offices – discarding irrelevant details as waves of information surge in over the equivalent of the Internet.
>
> Or to wait, unseen, unheard, unsmelt, in blizzard. Clothed in thermals but damp, imperfectly fed and uncomfortable, staring through a starlight scope sophisticated image intensifier to see in the dark in order to terminate a life by delivering a bullet with clinical precision or to bring medical aid to malnourished children, screaming in a vile, sweating hell beneath a sun-roasted tin roof."[25]

This is an interesting passage, especially from the point of view of our topic. It makes a striking juxtaposition between a number of military tasks and scenarios, and is structured as a sequence of ascending intensity of language, starting with the role of 'ambassador', the bearer of 'sacred artefacts', but culminating with blizzards, killing and 'vile, sweating hell'. The inclusive 'he or she' becomes progressively less visible in this sequence. The passage raises a question as to the implications of these developments for women's roles in the military, the nature of military tasks, and finally the gendered nature of militarism. But it does not answer this question, because it rolls all these developments into a single rhetorical sweep. It is necessary to unpack and examine them.

NEW TECHNOLOGY

As Bellamy makes clear, the place of technology in modern and future warfare is an aspect of current developments whose implications for the role of women is in some ways the least problematic. It means that soldiers, at least those from advanced industrial nations, will increasingly need technological skills rather than physical strength. Physical risk will also be much reduced. The business of the Armed

Forces has actually been highly technical for a long time. The straightforward infantry soldier is in the minority and, as Bellamy argues, the trade of the infantry soldier is itself increasingly technical. If, as Bellamy envisages, in the short to medium term the modern Armed Forces will continue to be supplied with unmanned systems and troops will to some extent be replaced by machines (during the Gulf War there was widespread use of robotic devices in place of manned vehicles and unmanned Pioneer drones were used to find Iraqi targets on the Kuwaiti coast) there can be few objections to technically competent female personnel operating such devices.[26] If, in future wars, robotic devices will indeed be able to undertake many of the functions associated with the Armed Forces of the past, while still remaining reliant on human brains for control, those brains can, presumably, be male or female.

The existence of a feminist argument to the effect that technology is itself gendered, which is an argument whose scope ranges from eco-feminism to discussions about women's access to and use of 'warlike' computer games and other domestic entertainment technology, does render somewhat less secure the straightforward inference from technology to parity of treatment in the military.[27] Nevertheless, the increasing use of technology serves quite adequately to overcome the more simplistic of arguments about women's capacities.

THE OBJECTIONS.

Advocates of greater access to the military by women need to contend with a set of arguments asserting its unfeasibility. Many of these, as already suggested, follow very familiar lines. Others are somewhat more specific to the particular context, meriting more extended treatment. Certainly in the category of 'familiar' are arguments which pertain to physical and mental capacities. Many such arguments could have been borrowed with little modification from debates over women's right to vote, or to join the police or the judiciary.

The response of Liberal feminists is a simple one: that while there may be differences in capacities between the genders, these are by no means as large as they have traditionally been taken to be, and moreover, that there is a zone of overlap sufficiently wide to rule out the possibility of categorical exclusions of women on grounds such as muscular strength or indeed pregnancy. It is now for example unlawful to dismiss women from the services simply on the grounds of pregnancy.

More peculiar to the military context are issues connected with morale. Difficulties supposedly created by the possibility of sexual or romantic relationships among front-line troops of mixed gender (which have also recently been aired, of course, in connection with the question of homosexuality) are among the questions at issue here. (It is worth noting here that in March, 1996 when the British Ministry of Defence recommended no change in the ban on homosexuals in the military, the Conservative Armed Forces Minister, Mr Nicholas Soames, told the House of Commons that a 'relaxation of the prohibition would damage operational effectiveness, leading to breaches of trust at critical moments and loss of morale'.)[28]

Such anxieties involve a very high estimation of the power and the disruptive potential of sexual desire. While it is possible to conjure up vivid scenarios in which military function is disrupted by uncontrollable and untimely urges and sexual jealousies, the plausibility of these scenarios needs to be questioned. Considerable doubt is cast on the anxiety they stem from by noting that military training already faces, apparently with some success, very considerable challenges posed by 'natural' human urges – of which fear and the urge for self-preservation are perhaps the most powerful. Ample testimony reports that combat activity in the military is not totally divorced from potentially intrusive human constraints such as fear and friendship. Military training works instead to channel, not to eliminate, such aspects of motivation.

The problem of morale is not, however, exhausted by the issue of sexuality. The presence of women in combat situations is taken by some analysts as threatening to transform battle into parody. The historian of war, Martin van Creveld has argued that

"Throughout history men have resented having to perform a woman's role as an insult to their manhood, even to the point where it was sometimes inflicted as a punishment: that they had been forced to fight at the side of, and against women, then either the affair would have turned into mock war – a common amusement in many cultures – or else they would have put down their arms in disgust...One suspects, that should they ever be faced with such a choice, men might very well give up women before they give up war."[29]

There are other perhaps more convincing arguments in terms of morale against a female presence. These are most powerfully articulated in the debate over whether women should be allowed to participate in front-line combat. At the moment women in the British services are barred from those tasks which might require them to 'close with and kill the enemy'. It has been argued that even, perhaps especially, in combat, male soldiers will feel the need to protect fellow female soldiers and competence suffers as a result of having to 'protect' female comrades as well as fight an enemy. In short, combat efficiency would be affected by the presence of women.[30]

A second argument used against placing women in a combat role is that both military and civilian morale might be undermined if the enemy launched a successful attack on female soldiers or if a female soldier was captured let alone subjected to sexual assault whilst held by the enemy. Indeed, during the Gulf War there was much speculation in the United States over the 'fate' and treatment of those female service personnel held captive by the Iraqis. As one journalist phrased it, for women 'attaining equality may carry a terrible price'. Leaving aside the fact that this was a price apparently acceptable for male soldiers it also subscribed to the notion of women as the 'protected'.[31]

What exactly is the issue here? The arguments against the participation of women in terms of morale are somewhat contradictory. Some predict the presence of women will cause a general de-motivation; others a distraction; others imply that a new and uncontrollable level of motivation to attack the enemy will result from violence against women comrades. Seemingly, when women are around, anything can happen. It is difficult to disentangle these arguments from more general depictions of women's role in society. Undoubtedly the vagueness of the concept of 'morale' contributes to this lack of clarity. Understood as some mysterious quality attaching to groups of soldiery, it lends itself to speculations about its fragility and unpredictability but also to constructions which necessarily build upon notions of male bonding and male friendship as necessary prerequisites to military efficiency.

Alternatively, morale may, we suggest, be understood in terms of military missions and the training and socialisation appropriate to them. Solidarity with the group is an important component, but the scope of the group in question varies widely, from the nation all the way down to the smallest unit – with some missions requiring levels of individual initiative incompatible even with this. Readiness to face risk is also an important quality, but again one about which it is impossible to generalise given the variety of possible military missions. Various kinds of antipathy or hostility may similarly be an aspect of morale with different levels of functionality in different circumstances. Training which creates the possibility of access to brutal behaviour, and thus establishes a certain volatility, may be more appropriate to some missions and roles in the military than others.

All of these considerations, and many others, show how difficult it is to speak of morale as a singular quality and how difficult it is to predict how the inclusion of women in, for example, combat roles may in reality affect the nature of the military.

Yet, views of women as necessarily detrimental to morale and efficiency continue to be articulated by those who determine policy particularly in respect of combat forces. The Chief of the Defence Staff, General Sir Charles Guthrie, for example, argued only recently that he was not sure that the nation was ready for the women in combat and ...that anyway he would not countenance such a step if it were to damage the effectiveness of the Armed Forces.[32] Leaving aside the fact that little, if any, evidence has been cited as to whether or not 'the nation' is 'ready' for women in combat, even if it were true, the national view would prove irrelevant if policy makers are determined that operational effectiveness in war will, in the short to medium term, still outweigh legal or political arguments over equality.

WOMEN AND NEW MISSIONS

Yet, the issues surrounding the set of developments which might be collectively termed 'new missions' or 'new wars' are complex – not least in respect of their implications for female participation and the gendered nature of militarism. Christopher Bellamy, in the quotation referred to earlier in this piece, alludes to these as if they were part of a single package of changes. Yet a robotic warrior controlling a hi-tech battlefield is not the only kind of soldier demanded by current trends.

New wars involve the increasing use of military forces in what might be termed 'muscular liberalism': the imposition of liberal values such as democracy and inter-ethnic toleration by (or at least with potential recourse to) armed force. This undoubtedly imposes on militaries a large range of new tasks – tasks whose character diminishes the contrast between civilian and military concerns, thus civilianising or (to use a more provocative term) 'feminising' the tasks of the military. Tasks such as conciliation and negotiation become, in this environment, not separate duties undertaken by specialised personnel for which the military simply clears the ground and secures the perimeter, but rather are integrated into the day-to-day operations of potentially all military personnel.

Such tasks, PSO, obviously create further opportunities for the integration of women. To say this is not necessarily to endorse the view of some feminists (and many traditionalist men too) that women are uniquely qualified as nurturers and conciliators. But if such a view resonates at all with the assumptions and values of the populations into which military PSO has intervened, the presence of women is, by virtue of these assumptions and values alone, likely to be a factor operating in favour of mitigating or reducing conflict. At a minimum, it is clear that increasing requirements to undertake such tasks further reduce the force of traditional objections to the participation of women in the full range of military duties.

The participation of women in these new missions has a

further advantage salient in the new context: it contributes to the legitimisation of military intervention for the home audience. More precisely, it avoids the obvious contradiction that might arise from dispatching forces that feature and express social exclusions, as well perhaps as displaying the results of socialisation into misogynistic values, on assignments whose purpose is the establishment, restoration or preservation of liberal and supposedly universal values. A seemingly paradoxical concomitant of the decentring of militaries from society has been increasing scrutiny of their activities by the media, and thus increasing attention by political leaders to the management of image in relation to the dispatching of military forces. Contradictions such as the one just mentioned will be increasingly difficult to sustain especially for a country such as the United Kingdom which claims to operate an 'ethical dimension' in its foreign policy.

So, if Western militaries are increasingly to wage war at a distance or operate as conciliators or mediators between estranged ethnic factions, there will remain few convincing arguments against the full inclusion of women. As Bellamy has argued, with the contraction of armed forces, commanders and ambitious army officers either male or female will have to demonstrate a range of skills, not necessarily those which have been traditionally associated with promotion in the Armed Forces. With the growth of Western military engagement in peace operations and the business of post-war reconstruction, military attachments to aid agencies will become increasingly common and increasingly valued.[33]

Already there are many similarities between the work of military units engaged in post-war Bosnia and the work of many non-governmental organisations. The skills needed for peace operations will be increasingly valued within the military and appointments in a zone of 'real' conflict will in time provide the basis for promotion for both female and male soldiers. What this all indicates is that given the modern tasks of the military, especially in terms of new technologies and missions, the question of the gender of soldiers within the armed services of the United Kingdom should become of much less significance.

NEW LIMITATIONS

Do these developments therefore represent imminent success for the Liberal feminist critique? The answer is yes. Not only this, but even a resolution of the contradictory aspects of that critique might seem to have become possible. For new technology and new missions make feasible, to an unprecedented degree, the involvement of women in the full range of military tasks and, arguably, make it desirable also. At the same time, the changing nature of military missions lends a significantly different meaning to 'militarism'.

However, there is occasion for doubting the view of current developments, especially in terms of military tasks and missions, that offers to permit this outcome. The key problems are these: *can* militaries perform this new range of tasks, and why should *militaries* perform them? Are military institutions, however modified (for instance by the full incorporation of women) capable of combining the new range of duties with those features which account for their being involved at all – namely the continued presence of physical threat and the continued need for decisive violent response to it?

During PSO, for example in the early years of the engagement in Bosnia, soldiers ensure that humanitarian aid is delivered and that lawyers, doctors and diplomats can go about their business in the reconstruction of war torn societies. Yet, as the example of Bosnia demonstrated only too clearly, Peace Support Operations can quickly cross the line into limited war with a corresponding shift in military missions. By 1995, UN forces had identified the Serbs as the enemy and western troops initially charged with the delivery of humanitarian aid were actually involved in a war with the Serbs.[34]

The US intervention in Somalia provides further stark illustrations of the resort to violence in the context of a 'humanitarian' mission.[35] The Battle of the Red Sea, as it became known, resulted in 18 American soldiers and over 500 Somalis being killed. What this means is that although the traditional picture of war has been transformed and the way in which certain groups such as women relate to war has at least in the Western world changed, there are still requirements for militaries, or parts of the Armed Forces, to engage in the violent types of combat which require a particular set of attributes.

Military personnel may increasingly be called upon to serve as diplomats and judges and in other quasi-civilian capacities. But there are good reasons why actual diplomats and judges are not deployed in the relevant situations. The military retains key features which make it uniquely necessary to these missions: its mobility, and above all its ability to engage in violence in order to bring violence under control. It is, whatever the mission and however it is represented to domestic political audiences, still required to have what Charles Townsend called the 'faith to kill'.[36]

The new missions of the military do not therefore necessarily just replace the old, but massively supplement them. So massively indeed that one can doubt whether the combination of tasks can be reliably effected – and indeed there are examples both of over-zealous and of over-tardy resort to traditional military responses by personnel in peacekeeping or intervention roles.[37]

The proliferation of tasks makes it less easy than ever before to generalise about the kinds of training and socialisation, and the kind of people, that militaries require. It is already questionable that the command structure of military forces can combine the requirement for decisive and violent action with that for tact, conciliation and the tolerance of ambiguity, loss of face and so on that accompanies PSO. It is surely asking too much that the combination should be expected of all military personnel. There will, as always, be tasks that require forms of socialisation and ways of maintaining morale which will never be compatible with the liberal values the tasks are actually supposed to defend. In these respects, an irreducible core of military function is irredeemably gendered.

Perhaps these sorts of tasks will become more covert – not only for the obvious operational reasons but also for reasons of image management for the domestic audience. In this respect the contribution of such 'masculine' activities to the perpetuation of cultural patriarchy may be further minimised. To this extent, the factors we have mentioned – technological warfare, legitimisation, the quasi-civilian aspects of missions such as PSO – will indeed contribute to the successful resolution of the Liberal feminist critique. But we contend that not only feminists but all those who would celebrate the imminent arrival of clean wars, good wars, and most of all peaceable wars are indulging at least in part, in a kind of denial. Warfare may no longer be the grisly abattoir that it was on the battlefields of World War I, but it will always contain actions and moments from which we in Liberal democratic societies will be strongly inclined and able to avert our gaze.

THE PROBLEMS OF PREDICTING

In this respect, it is likely that in the short to medium term, women will increasingly be recruited into the armed services not least because of the problems in recruiting servicemen and the demands of employment legislation. Liberal feminists have, therefore, fought and won certain political and social 'battles'. However, it is not difficult to predict that certain missions and elements of the services, particularly cap badged posts in the infantry or the Royal Marines, will remain closed to female soldiers. These exclusions of course run counter to existing norms within liberal democracies which rightly cherish notions of full equality in employment. But there are a number of hurdles to be overcome before what we might term 'full access' for women in the military will or could be achieved. While there is little doubt that female personnel can and do play increasingly crucial roles in PSO, (note here too the recent deployment of women to serve in Northern Ireland) the problems of 'physical' capacity, despite RMA, for some of the more specialised combat missions still remains.

There is also the challenge of what we can term the 'morale' issue. While we have pointed to the complexity of the very concept of morale, if senior members of the services as well as ordinary soldiers feel threatened or undermined by mixed gender units, and there is evidence that this remains the case, there will necessarily be a gap between what society might demand and what is effective or cohesive on the ground.[38] While training and conscious raising might over time eradicate some of these problems and radicalise organisational culture, whether it can do so totally remains a moot point. Indeed, here of course the opposition to mixed gender units, of the families of those who serve, has been well documented.[39] Given the existing problems of recruitment and retention within the services, these objections will also have to be taken seriously and addressed.

Overall then, there is no question that women will continue to serve in increasing numbers in the armed services of the United Kingdom. Demography, social norms and legislation will ensure greater efforts on the part of the services to oversee the recruitment, retention and promotion of women while RMA and PSO will ensure a more challenging range of tasks available to women. Yet, issues of morale and what might or might not be regarded as 'old fashioned' or macho concerns over women in combat will also ensure that the issue of women on the front line will not be resolved quickly.

NOTES

1. Feminists who have written and debated on women and military service can be categorised in two ways. Feminists located in the first generally adopt a Pacifist view and express dismay at the interest in women joining the armed services. The second tradition however has produced groups of feminists who use what are termed 'rights based' arguments to push for the greater inclusion of women in the military. We term this the Liberal Feminist tradition. On this distinction see Laura L. Miller, 'Feminism and the Exclusion of Army Women from Combat' in *Gender Issues*, Vol.16, No.3. Summer 1998. pp.33–63. On varieties of feminism generally see for example Linda Nicholson (ed.), *The Second Wave: A Reader in Feminist Theory* (New York and London: Routledge, 1997); Imelda Whelehan, *Modern Feminist Thought: From the Second Wave to 'Post-Feminism'* (Edinburgh University Press, 1995); Paul Byrne, *Social Movements in Britain* (London and New York: Routledge, 1997) Ch. 7.
2. Jill Steans, *Gender and International Relations: An Introduction* (London: Polity, 1998) pp.81–89. For a fuller discussion of the issues raised on women and war, see Caroline Kennedy-Pipe, 'Women in the Military.' in *Journal of Strategic Studies*, Vol.23, No.4. December 2000, pp.23–51. See also Cynthia Enloe, *Maneuvers The International Politics of Militarizing Women's Lives* (Berkeley and Los Angeles, University of California Press, 2000) p.29.
3. Steans, op. cit.
4. Ibid. p. 84.
5. M.B. Davie, *The Evolution of War: A Study of Its Role in Early Societies* (New Haven, CT: Yale University Press, 1929).
6. Norman Dixon, *On the Psychology of Military Incompetence* (London: Basic Books, 1976) pp.208–218.
7. Penny Stanley, 'Mass Rape in War: Feminist Thought and British Press Representations of the Balkan Conflict, 1991-1995', unpublished Ph.D. thesis, UCW, Aberystwyth, 1998. See also Ruth Seifert, 'The Second Front: The Logic of Sexual Violence in Wars', in *Women's Studies International Forum*, Vol.19, Nos. 1/2, January/April 1996.
8. Catherine Nicarchos, 'Woman, War and Rape: Challenges Facing the

International Tribunal for the Former Yugoslavia', in *Human Rights*, Vol. 17, 1995, pp.668–671. See also Caroline Kennedy-Pipe and Penny Stanley, 'Mass Rape in War: the Balkan Wars', in Ken Booth, *The International Journal of Human Rights*, Special Issue *The Kosovo Tragedy: The Human Rights Dimensions*, Vol 4, Nos. 3/4 Autumn/Winter 2000, pp.67–87.

9.   Denise Aydelott, 'Mass Rape During War: Prosecuting Bosnian Rapists Under International Law' in *Emory Law Review*, Vol. 7, No. 2, Fall 1993, pp.585–631.

10. Michael S. Sherry, *In the Shadow of War: The United States since the 1930s* (New Haven and London: Yale University Press, 1995), p.195.

11. Steans, op. cit, p.100.

12. For a brief analysis of the feelings of the regular soldier on the way to war, see John Keegan, *War and Our World: the Reith Lectures, 1998* (London : Hutchinson, 1998) p.54.

13. On the issue of morale, see Rosanna Hertz, 'Guarding Against Women? Responses of Military Men and Their Wives to Gender Integration' in *Journal of Contemporary Ethnography*, Vol. 25, No.2, July 1996, pp.251–284.

14. Judith Hicks Stiehm, *Arms and the Enlisted Woman* (Philadelphia: Temple University Press, 1989). See also Hicks Stiehm, 'The Protected, the Protector, the Defender' in J.H. Stiehm (ed.) *Women and Men's Wars* (Oxford: Paragon, 1982). See also Lorry M. Fenner, 'Either You Need These Women or You do Not: Informing the Debate on Military Service and Citizenship' in *Gender Issues*, Vol.16. No.3, Summer 1998. pp.5–32.

15. Most of the troops who saw ground combat in Vietnam came from poor, working class, rural, or lower middle class backgrounds. The more privileged could usually escape service through deferments for attending college or for service in the reserves. See Sherry, *In the Shadow of War* op. cit. pp.295–297.

16. See for example, Antonia Fraser, *The Weaker Vessel: Woman's Lot in Seventeenth-century England* (London: Arrow, 1999). See also Svetlana Alexeivich, '"I am Loath to Recall." Russian Women's Service in World War II', in *Women's Studies Quarterly*, Nos. 3 & 4, 1995, pp.78–84.

17. Jean Bethke Elshtain, *Women and War* (New York: Basic Books, 1987).

18. Christopher Dandeker and Mady Wechsler Segal, 'Gender Integration in Armed Forces: Recent Policy Developments in the United Kingdom' in *Armed Forces and Society*, Vol.23, 1996, pp.29–47. On the strategies employed by national militaries for recruitment, see Enloe, op. cit.

19. Ibid.

20. Edwin Dorne, 'A Considered Opinion: Integrating Women into the Military' in *The Brookings Review* Vol. 10, No. 4, Fall, 1992 p.5. See also 'Women in the Military' at http//www/pafb.at.mil.deom1/wommil95.htm

21. See Dandeker, op. cit.

22. House of Commons Defence Committee Report, Session 2000–2001. The Strategic Defence Review, Policy for People. HC. 29. Vol.1.

23. Edward N. Luttwak, 'Towards Post-Heroic Warfare', in *Foreign Affairs*, Vol. 74, No.3, May–June 1995, pp. 109–122.

24. Jean Baudrillard, *The Gulf War* (London: Power Publishers, 1995).

25. Christopher Bellamy, *Knights in White Armour: The New Art of War and Peace* (London: Pimlico, 1997) p.195.

26. Ibid.

27. See for example Joni Seager, *Earth Follies: Feminism, Politics and the Environment* (London: Earthscan, 1993); Karen J. Warren with Barbara Wells-Howe, *Ecological Feminism* (London and New York: Routledge, 1994); Judy Wajcman, *Feminism Confronts Technology* (University Park, PA:

Pennsylvania University Press, 1991); Ann Gray, *Video Playtime: The Gendering of a Leisure Activity* (London: Routledge, 1992).

28. 'Minister Stands Firm Against Gays in the Military', *The Guardian*, 5 March 1996. Quoted in Enloe op. cit. p.29.

29. Martin van Creveld, *The Transformation of War* (New York: Free Press, 1991) pp.218–23. See also Martin van Creveld, 'Less than We Can Be: Men, Women and the Modern Military,' in *Journal of Strategic Studies*, Vol.23, No.4, December 2000, pp.1–21

30. M.C. Devilbis, 'Gender Integration and Unit Deployment: A Study of GI Joe', in *Armed Forces and Society*, Vol. 11, No. 4, Summer 1985, p.538.

31. See 'Women in the Military: The First POW', in *Newsweek*, 11 February 1991. Quoted in Cynthia Nantais and Martha F. Lee, 'Women in the United States Military: protectors or protected? The Case of prisoner of war Melissa Rathbun-Nealy' in *Journal of Gender Studies*, Vol.8, No.2, July 1999, pp.183–191. See also J. Wheelwright, '"It was Exactly Like the Movies!" The Media's Use of the Feminine during the Gulf War', in C. Addis, V. Russo and L. Sebesta (eds.), *Women Soldiers: Images and Realities* (New York: St Martin's Press, 1994).

32. Michael Smith, 'Guthrie Launches Final Assault on 'PC' Forces.' *Daily Telegraph*, 16 February 2001.

33. Bellamy, op.cit. p.195. Michael Ignatieff, *The Warrior's Honor, Ethnic War and the Modern Conscience* (London: Vintage, 1998)

34. Lawrence Freedman, 'Bosnia: Does Peace Support Make Any Sense?', in *NATO Review*, No.6, November 1995, pp.19–23; David Rieff, 'The Lessons of Bosnia, Morality and Power' in *World Policy Journal*, Vol.12, No.1, Spring 1995, pp.76–88.

35. Mark Bowden, *Black Hawk Down* (New York: Atlantic Monthly Press, 1999).

36. Charles Townsend, 'Fin de Siècle', in Alex Danchev (ed.), *Fin de Siècle: The Making of the Twentieth Century* (London and New York: I.B. Tauris, 1995).

37. Bowden, op. cit.

38. See Dandeker and Segal, op. cit.

39. See Hertz, op. cit.

6

Moral Component – The 'Regimental System'

PATRICK MILEHAM
University of Paisley

THE BRITISH WAY

We have been very slack in many areas of research on the British Army. Nearly twenty years ago General Sir John Hackett in 1983, expressed a wish that:

> "Some day I want to turn the ethnologists on to a study of the regimental system as a means of strengthening group resistance to stress. Their advice may well be that instead of a quaint and decorative traditional survival, we have in the British regimental system a military instrument of deadly efficiency."[1]

This highly functional, cavalry/armoured/airborne commander and university chancellor's wish has never been acted upon.

A few years later the then Chief of the General Staff confirmed that the British regimental system was a 'priceless asset and one not rightly to be cast aside'.[2] The view of a less senior officer, writing in *The British Army Review* shortly after, was that

> "In the end, there are few absolutes in this splendid regimental system of which we are all part. It has its weaknesses, but they are far outweighed by its great strengths. It is gloriously inconsistent between its parts for good reason. But of its critical importance there can be no doubt."[3]

Antony Beevor's conclusion a year later was that 'The real family has at last become more important than its military substitute.'[4] Confusing the situation, however, von Zugbach and Dietz, dwell on notions of prestige and tradition, the former on the residual anti-egalitarianism of the system, the latter gloomily ending, 'it is essential now that the trappings of an obsolete system are not retained at the expense of the vital spirit'.⁵ Neither author, however, identifies what that vital spirit was or is.

More recently, in 1994, Colonel C. W. Paskell, at the Royal Military College of Science/Cranfield University, discovered many of the strengths of the regimental system just as 'Options for Change' brought about not only changes (cuts) in the Combat Arms (formerly 'Teeth Arms'), but reorganised the Combat Service Support Arms as well. With regards to the management science and the sociology of the system, he concluded that:

> "The regimental system is essentially sound and useful. It is not well understood within the Army, or only instinctively. The main purpose is the legitimacy and survival of the Army in peacetime, for which it is well adapted but not necessarily remaining so, given the changing [defence] environment."⁶

The fact that the British Army 'instinctively' maintained its regimental system during a golden age between the years of 1956 (date of the last British politico-military failure) and 1989 (fall of the Berlin Wall), is now part of history. The fact that the British Army discovered or re-discovered doctrine in the latter mentioned year, with *Design for Military Operations. The British Military Doctrine*, is also of great significance. Notably 'military effectiveness' and 'fighting power' were recognised as not being categorically the same (in Aristotle's scheme of categories) in this definitive document. Percipiently the authors drew the distinction between the 'physical component' – the means to fight, the 'conceptual component' – the thought process and the 'moral component' – the ability to get people to fight.⁷

A little over a decade later, after major structural changes to the Army, together with a rethinking about military power as significant as any in peacetime since the Army's inception in 1660, where stands the British regimental system today? In my opinion, drawing the connection between the 'unit' of military effectiveness/fighting power and the Army's intuitive conception of the moral component reinforces both.

71

In adopting this approach and agreeing with Colonel Paskell about the Army's understanding of the regimental system being 'instinctive', I must add that I believe that the articulation and understanding of the moral component itself needs considerable strengthening.

BONDING AND BRANDING – THE REAL REGIMENT

It might surprise many a modern-day officer that contractorisation and budget holding is nothing new to the British Army. 'New Management Strategy' and the system which includes the lowest level of budget holders, restored a long standing managerial tradition of military decentralisation. An Army has three basic functions, fighting, regeneration and preparation for war. From 1660 it was the private enterprise of those commissioned by the monarch who saw to these three functions, not the centralised institution of a national Army which was constitutionally illegal. Regeneration, historians will add, was not always easy and unpreparedness for war the norm.

The post-Crimea and Indian Mutiny reforms of Edward Cardwell and Hugh Childers had the effect of centralising the Army more effectively for war-fighting, but confirmed and strengthened the decentralised regeneration function of the regiments and corps of the Army. These two Secretaries for War consolidated the Army, beginning with the 'localisation' exercise in 1873, and ending with the incorporation of the twin regular battalions of infantry, with militia and rifle volunteer battalions, into a new system of regimentation in 1881. The purpose was, above all, to provide for continuity in peacetime as well as war. In the then prevailing conception of military power, manning overseas garrisons and fighting small colonial wars, less than 25% of the Army (regular and reserve) was committed overseas at any one time. The 'Regiment' of infantry was self-sustaining and all the regiments added together, comprised more than two thirds of the of the Army's total strength. The test of the system came in 1899, when the nation fielded a 'continental army' to preserve the integrity of the Empire from the Boers. It was a dress-rehearsal for what was to follow. The Haldane reforms of 1906–1909 centralised the system more closely, just in time.

It was between 1871 and 1914 that what I call the 'Real

Regiment' rose to prominence. After the abolition of purchase of commissions and promotions (1871), individual officers were tied to an individual infantry or cavalry regiment for all their career. Staff appointments were for the few who took risks with their regimental career, as were those who sought to transfer to another regiment. These factors greatly strengthened the concept of regiment, even if its members would not at the time have recognised the expression. Individual regiments became truly 'closed societies'. The unit of fighting power was confirmed as the battalion. Having two in each regiment was a triumph of good sense. The regimental left brain/right brain dichotomy provided for internal competition, flexibility for posting, including trickle posting and in case individuals needed a second chance to shine, without losing caste.

To see the real regiment through modern eyes, first one should turn to what I consider is the best model of the closed society – Goffman's concept of the 'Total Institution'.[8] Goffman's view is that total institutions are characterised by the differentiation between 'staff and inmates'; the 'us' and 'them' in this case being between officers/NCOs and private soldiers respectively. Officers legitimated the power of the NCOs, and together they governed and disciplined the soldiery. Other characteristics are:

> "mortification processes...A privilege system of rewards and punishments...house rules...institutional lingo...social formalities and informalities' [and the] phenomenon of...engaging in forbidden activity"[9].

The latter includes the sub-cultures, which in regiments usually escape the notice of officers, but not necessarily NCOs.

Goffman notes that,

1. "All aspects of life are conducted in the same place, ...and under the same single authority.

2. ...daily activity...carried out in the immediate company of a large batch of others...

3. ...the day's activities are tightly scheduled...imposed from above...

4.   ...the contents of the various enforced activities are brought together as parts of a single overall rational plan, purportedly designed to fulfil the official aims of the institution."[10]

Life is totally institutional and, in a word, regimented.

Modern terminology would have it that the regiment was the means of 'bonding' and 'branding'. It was the creation of a system within a system, a closed society within the Army's closed society. The regiment and its battalions were competitive, exclusive, jealous of their honour, demanding of loyalty, and if in 1881 they had no striking character or idiosyncrasies already, quickly developed them. Regional affiliation based on the county town depot, history of battles and regimental heroes, distinction of uniform and accoutrements (usually of practical origin, often extravagant), of which the 'colours' became symbols of regimental integrity and sacrifice – all these facts and factors combined to distinguish one proud regiment from another, into a system of deadly military efficiency.

Distinct from numerous volumes of regimental hagiography, one of the best regimental histories is Sir John Baynes's *Morale, a Study of Men and Courage*.[11] Baynes wrote about one battalion in 1914 and its first battle in the First World War. A regimental son of the Cameronians (Scottish Rifles), he analysed the Regiment's traditions, or what would now be termed its culture, in terms of regimental spirit (*esprit de corps*) and morale; the discipline in general and that particular to the battalion; the internal relationships among the soldiers, NCOs and officers as three distinct groups; the 'regimental officer', his social standing, duties and way of life; together with other matters such as 'religion and morals', 'patriotism' and the relationship with 'High Command and the Staff'. The 2nd Scottish Rifles, as exemplars of the regimental system, were put in context with the then prevailing class system in Britain and socio-economic backgrounds of members of the regiment. Baynes concluded that the most important factors fostering high morale were,

"pride in regiment...excellent officer-other rank relationships, ...strong discipline...The balance between self-discipline and the imposed sort... The sense of duty of all ranks; highly developed in the officer by his training ... [and] sound administration."[12]

As they marched on 10 March 1915 to their first battle, an almost perfectly integrated body of men, Baynes reminds the reader that, within the 2nd Scottish Rifles, 'these are living men: the knowledge that so many will be dead within a few hours, gave the picture a bitter poignance'.[13] Thirteen officers and 112 other ranks were killed, 344 of the remainder were wounded or missing. Tragically, high losses in war are often caused by high morale.[14]

The truth is that, while putting on the appearance of being a military 'machine' to impress the enemy and for self-confidence, fighting units were and remain highly 'organic' institutions. Behind their mechanistic facade, they are collectively very vulnerable, psychologically as well as physically.

It should not escape the reader's notice that the Cameronians, the first battalion of the regiment, were the original divinely-inspired 'covenanters'. Today's explanation of the 'moral component' of military effectiveness is entitled Soldiering. *The Military Covenant*.[15] Indeed generations of soldiers have put faith and even quasi-religious belief in their regiment's immortality, vital, literally, in an institution whose primary function might bring them intimately close to danger and death. The 'colours', 'standards' and 'guidons' were and still are icons, consecrated by an ordained minister of the church during a ceremonial parade combined with a religious service. Traditionally they are defended to the death. The battalion system, subdividing members of the same regiment into fighting units, ensured continuation and the ability for regeneration. Above all, regiments took on individual characters, as well as characteristics, emphasising that they were intensely human institutions.

I do not think it over the top to ascribe the term *Realmilitär*[16] to such a system. The best of the system and the best of the regiments provided for their members some inner numinous strength, with the outward manifestations of charismatic reputation and honour. Individuals did not merely hold values, they utterly believed in their regiment and their fighting duty within the great scheme of things military. Vulnerable physically, their psychological strength lay in their supremely unquestioning faith. If this seems unsophisticated and strange to us, then it is we who are the military agnostics.

In my opinion the apogee of both the regiment and the regimental system in the British Army was August 1914. Regular, militia and volunteer battalions mobilised simultaneously. It is unlikely that the subsequent and unprecedented experiment of mass voluntary enlistment would have worked so well, if it were not based on the 'real regiment', the existing 'total institution', more or less ready for the first 'total war' experience of the nation.

NEO-REGIMENT AND QUASI-REGIMENT

Mobilisation in 1914 immediately incorporated the territorial and reserve (formerly Militia) battalions into neo-total institutions of the regular Army. This could not, however, be deemed pure, simple, wholly 'total' fighting units like the 'real battalions' of the regular army: individuals had other existences than military. Other classifications of neo-battalions were the 'Kitchener' battalions of existing regiments, and locally recruited 'Pals' battalion, who came as already-formed groups of townsmen, workmates, sports clubs members and other groups, rather naively thinking they could take military service on their own terms, rather than that of the Army as total institution.

In the huge rush for voluntary recruitment, the existing regimental system provided a structure for generically expanding itself, which surprised even the Secretary of State for War, Lord Kitchener. Instantly a man took the loyal oath, and received his regimental number, he adopted:

- A military identity – for instilling a high degree of self-confidence.

- A feeling of being special, in an exclusive group, brought together for an important purpose – for comradeship and loyalty.

- An instant history, with battle honours – for a sense of continuity, even intimations of immortality.

- A uniform, with distinctive, symbols, badges and

accoutrements, marking his regiment's distinctiveness – instilling healthy internal army competition.

• An organisation which, in the event of his being wounded or killed, he believed he could rely on for support of himself and his family.

The British Expeditionary Force, comprising real battalions as total institutions, soon reinforced by reservists and territorials, bore the brunt of the first year's fighting in the First World War. The old type of soldiers and regimental officers were replaced by new, volunteer 'inmates' and 'staff' in the neo-battalions for the duration, whatever that meant for the individual. The regimental system had provided for the infantry a self-regenerating continuity of regimental manpower, wearing the 'real' capbadge and living as the 'real' regiment of their imagination, fighting and dying for their adopted spiritual values, their comrades and the great cause. The spirit, however, in many instances became more focused on the brigade or division, appropriate to the larger scale of operations. New drafts, upon new drafts, arrived from the regimental depots, replacing casualties upon casualties. Like the 'same river one can never step into twice', the battalions were regenerated time and time again, which also like the 'ever-rolling stream', vast numbers of its sons were borne away. Neo-battalions could and did fight as fiercely as any real-battalions, their self-sacrifice no less than the ultimate faithfulness to duty of the old regular army. Witness the 16th Manchesters' defence of Manchester Hill near St Quentin, on the Western Front during the desperate fighting of March 1918 – 'resistance to the last round and the last man. Here we fight and here we die',[17] ordered the CO. He meant it and they did.

So much for the neo-battalions and neo-regiments that emerged from the old pre-war Army.

Quasi-regiment is the term we can use for functional unit structures of consolidating artillery battalions and engineer squadrons between 1871 and 1918. Their business was not primarily closing with and killing the enemy. Sub-units and detachments were often widely dispersed. They, and other specialist corps, however, readily adopted the style, values and beliefs of the real regiment, albeit their value lay with larger groupings within the Army – brigades, divisions, army corps – in which they were incorporated: gunners would die to defend their guns, sappers proved faithful unto death in carrying out their often lonely front-line tasks. The loyalties tended to lie with immediate comrades and the concept of the larger 'corps' (or in the case of the Royal Artillery, nominally the Royal Regiment), signifying the whole as greater than the parts.

Other military functions and appropriate quasi-regiments and corps emerged during the century, the Tank Corps, Royal Signals, Parachute Regiment, Army Air Corps, Royal Electrical and Mechanical Engineers, as well as the Services, Royal Army Medical Corps, Royal Army Chaplains Department and Women's Royal Army Corps, to name some. Their strength lay primarily in their function, not of course discounting the spirit in which they actually performed their duties, arguably modelled on the best of the spirit of the real regiments of infantry and cavalry. They could not, however, be the 'total institutions' in function or on operations. They did not act necessarily in the same place, in large numbers, all doing the same activities. They worked to more flexible 'schedules' and a much greater single overall rational plan, particularly in mobile warfare, which characterised the years between 1939 and 1945.

The inter-war years were an uneasy period for the British Army. The real regiments more or less re-established their customs and spirit, albeit real continuity was lacking. Voluntary service all but disappeared. In 1939–45, numerous neo-battalions were raised and fought more or less successfully in European, desert and jungle campaigns. They were not the same as the totally absorbing institutions marking the 'fighting machine'[18] of 1914. A much higher proportion of the called-up conscripts were employed in the larger corps and new specialist units (e.g. anti-aircraft, anti tank, searchlight etc.) than hitherto. Small-group loyalty within infantry and armoured units became more important with the more dispersed nature of operations that developed.

The historian A. D. Harvey concluded, perhaps unfairly, that during the Second World War the, 'British soldier in his baggy khaki and shaving-bowl helmet looked perhaps the least military of all European soldiery of this war; equipped, fed and supported by the huge social effort...the British armed forces turned out to be something of a blunt instrument'.[19] In the same book, an unnamed general is quoted as saying. 'soldiers must be trained before they can fight, fed before they can march and relieved before they are worn out'.[20] The message of war preparation had been learnt the hard way.

Such statements are unfair to all fighting regiments in the war some of the time, and to some regiments, unfair for all of their war record. Correlli Barnett, however, observed that during the Second World War the regimental system actually broke down. 'It was impossible to solve the problem of drafts and reinforcements within self-contained regimental compartments.'[21] Regiments could no longer regenerate themselves as they did in the First World War. Small-group cohesion and loyalties, nevertheless, prevailed, the hall-mark of the quasi-regimental spirit. While we can agree with Barnett that the system broke down, clearly the regiments did not. They are still with us six decades later.

The history of the regiments in the all-professional Army (post 1960, the ending of conscription), shows a diversity within the system of much complexity. There are some self-authenticating real regiments,[22] although in truth all are quasi-regiments, because virtually all have been amalgamated, and have adopted an exaggerated history of descent and battle honours, particularly the 'large regiments' of infantry. All have been re-branded for each generation. The new Royal Logistic Corps and Adjutant General's Corps, perhaps should be designated neo-corps, until their novelty has worn off in a decade or two. The incorporation of women into all regiments and corps, except infantry and armour, takes the Army a step further away from the original male-bonding function of the real regiment. The trends for egalitarianism and political correctness has broken the once significant characteristic of the real regiment – its boasted 'exclusiveness'. The Army has moved inexorably away from the culture of the total institution. Individuals seemingly write their own terms and conditions of service. In garrisons, such as remain, the regiment has for decades taken on the 'large social effort', parallel to and yet much more effective than the welfare state.

In terms of soldiering, small-group cohesion has grown in importance in armoured formations as well as in the field of peace support operations. The modern doctrine of 'mission command', delegation of the 'commanders' intent' means that the corporal[23] is the most important person in the field. Private infantry soldiers routinely 'negotiate orders',[24] according to John Hockey's analysis of the early 1980s infantry, indicating an existential discipline was displacing faith in a belief-system. In battle groups, combat teams and other force structures comprising many 'capbadges', individuals carry with them the differentiation of 'their' original regiment, as a human reaction to the otherwise inhuman scale of today's 'military machine'. In all units there are, according to Charles Kirke, a number of largely hidden social anthropological structures sustaining fighting or functional spirit, which is the way the Army really works, as opposed to the official theory.[25]

At the present time, I suggest that the notion of regimental branding, still remains a feature, and much stronger than a mere trace element, of today's strangely centralised/decentralised British Army. The regiment means different things perhaps to career officers and NCOs than to short-term officers and soldiers. The old comrade tradition too, may well survive and inspire more generations to come. Recruiting is almost entirely a centralised activity, which is perhaps why it has failed in recent years effectively to regenerate the Field Army.

VIRTUAL REGIMENT

The greatest danger to the future of all human institutions qua institutions, is the computer. An 'agency' is an incorporation which has no life of its own other than what it does, unlike a regiment, a university college, a hospital, football club or even a government ministry. As bureaucracies improve, with the use of IT and budgetary regimes, they are drawn closer to Weber's ideal model. We wonder what the future of British regiments will be. Will they become mere agencies?

The British Army has already witnessed a synthetic war. Operation 'Granby' in 1991 was very real to the Iraqis, but somewhat surreal to British participants. Witness an NCO of the Royal Scots, interviewed for the Services Sound and Vision Corporation video:

"It's not like an exercise when you hear the contact [enemy firing]...you're paying a lot of attention to it...The guys in the back were pretty apprehensive. There's total isolation in the Warrior [armoured personnel carrier with 30mm cannon], total silence...there's an artificiality about it...get out of the vehicle and all hell is let loose.

We won the fire fight...gave the trenches a jolly good blasting...taking them out at 800m with HE. The difficulty was to make a decision to commit men to the ground [dismount] to clear trenches and take the surrender of the enemy. There was an indication that the enemy wanted to surrender. The company commander wanted to push forward...my worry was we were going too fast...going through trenches that we hadn't cleared. When we went in, there was relatively nothing for us to do...there wasn't the will to fight from the enemy."

So how will either the regiment or the regimental system, which are categorically different phenomena, survive the inexorable 'digitization of the battlespace'. 'Realistic simulations', Chris Hables Grey informs us,

'also serve as "a means of indoctrination" both because they serve to validate the system itself and because for a techo-soldier launching a missile, simulated conditions and real-war conditions are almost identical.'[26]

It is easy to suspend belief in such circumstances, but there is surely a difference between virtual reality and real reality.

Indeed the requirement of the virtual infantryman or crew member of the future, has been decided. Technology factors are already planned for the dismounted infantrymen, as he closes with and kills the enemy in future intense conflict. The Future Infantry System Technology (FIST) – a mind boggling range of portable military equipments – will be designed for him to be a walking (or running) technologically communicating, locating, navigating, reporting, intelligence-gathering, virtual reality observing, self-sustainable, cyber-space robot. Somehow he will still have to be a human being. While the pull is towards the 'total mechanistic' Army of the future, war and operations will induce the same apprehension felt by real, live human beings as in the Gulf War – at least until non-lethal weapons take over completely in some wargaming future, that will decide all human conflict, forever.

THE MORAL COMPONENT

Turning back the date to 1989, the year that doctrine was rediscovered, the moral component of military power was exposed in the literature, partly as a consequence of the codification of manoeuvre theory. Brigadier Richard Simpkin taught the value of 'moral' advantage over the enemy in his book *Race to the Swift* of 1985.[27] *British Military Doctrine* teaches that the new (to the British Army) concept and policy termed 'mission command' relies, among other factors, on complete 'mutual trust between commanders'[28] of different levels, down to and including corporals. Absolute mutual trust, it is argued, cannot be anything other than a moral military imperative, if mission command is to succeed to win wars or bring peace support operations to a successful conclusion. There can be no 'them' and 'us' division in fighting units. A decade on, officers with whom I speak are of two minds about the practical relevance of mission command in the digitised battlespace, but not about 'total' collective action.

I accept that military doctrine is 'what is taught',[29] but it is much more than that. It is the ability to draw on abstract theory, as a basis for arguing specific applications thereafter. Unlike the 'DS Pink' (the colloquial expression stating the opinion of the senior officer present must be obeyed), doctrine concerning the humanities, which includes warfare, properly exposes hypotheses, not categorical imperatives. Doctrine on the moral component, is expressed in the Army Doctrine Publication Volume 5, *Soldiering. The Military Covenant*. As a work of military metaphysics, with its catalogue of military virtues and articles of military faith, it cannot be faulted. Officers of 1914, regular, territorial and volunteer, would have applauded it. Field Marshals Slim, Wavell and Montgomery are quoted in it, as is Sir Basil Liddell Hart.

Soldiering, however, in my view, contains some categorical errors. The 'Core Values' chapter contains a commendable list of official aspirations, which nevertheless are a compounded mix of individual beliefs and behaviours together with corporate values, with no indication of psycho-philosophical differentiation.[30] They are:

> "morale, moral strength and just cause, values and standards of the Army, self-less commitment, courage, discipline (including self-discipline), integrity, loyalty respect for others, enduring characteristics, volunteer professionalism, corps and regimental spirit, the chain of command, leadership, the British Army."[31]

Soldiering also contains the Army's 'ethos statement',

> "That spirit which inspires soldiers to fight. It derives from, and depends upon the high degrees of commitment, self-sacrifice and mutual trust, 'which together are essential to the maintenance of morale."[32]

In my opinion there is a whole chapter missing, one which links the military and moral behaviour of soldiers with all of human life, public and private.

The 'Corps and Regimental spirit' section, has four 'key characteristics', being 'comradeship', 'example', 'pride' and 'flexibility'.[33] The latter would have been fiercely resisted in 1914, but is an imperative of modern-day 'force design'. 'Example' depends on awareness of the much-attenuated regimental histories or legends, but government policy currently seems intent, wittingly or not, on diminishing Britain's past and anything that appears to be a dark force from a previous age. 'Pride' is about exclusiveness, while 'comradeship' defines small-group loyalty, which to accord with government policy, implies 'inclusiveness'.

Putting *Soldiering. The Military Covenant* (and its two levels of summary) through critical analysis, the first limitation is that it represents military ideology, not necessarily reality. All the above-mentioned sections, considerations and virtues are variables, not constants. The assumption in the document is that they are the latter.

Second, the discussion does not include mention of the consequences of the legal changes which diminish the *Realmilitär* status of the British Army. This includes repeal in

1987 of Section 10 of the Crown Proceedings Act 1947, which allows servicemen and women to sue in the civil courts for a wide range of injury sustained while serving in the Armed Forces. Commanding officers' disciplinary powers, upon which their subordinates' practice of self-discipline rested, have been severely curtailed by recent changes to *Army Summary Jurisdiction Regulations*. These provisions and the incorporation of the European Convention on Human Rights and Fundamental Freedom into British law by the Human Rights Act of 2000, without derogation of any articles inappropriate for the 'unique nature of soldiering', puts on notice the 'unlimited liability [of servicemen] to give their lives'.[34]

These legal alterations to military discipline fail the Army's own 'Service Test' contained in the *Values and Standards* code, in that the changes 'are likely to impact on the efficiency or operational effectiveness of the Army'. *Soldiering. The Military Covenant* will either have to be substantially re-written, or all the above legal changes repealed or subjected to a realistic derogation plan.

THE EXISTENTIALIST REGIMENT

As Bernard Levin once remarked, 'the future is not the same as it was'. One can confirm that this comment applies to the British Army. For a start, looking ahead at military regimes of 2030, the efficacy of decentralised authority in manoeuvrist doctrine may appear to deconstruct the whole idea of military cohesion. Leo Tolstoy, a veteran of the Crimean War, discovered that military thinking is really algebraic,[35] in that it has to take account of countless variables in human behaviour and the circumstances and events in war. The corporal is in algebraic communion with his platoon commander, his commanding officer and his commander-in-chief. The actions of each commander is as significant, albeit in their own way, as every other.

A well-led military unit, section, platoon, company, battalion or equivalent is self-regenerating in a very different way from merely recruiting and training up new members. I refer to the regeneration of up-and-coming 'leaders',[36] the next generation, which on operations may be needed instantly to replace casualties (injured, dead or promoted).

An infantry section will generate its next leaders within a short space of time, even in peacetime. The battalion, currently configured, may take fifteen to twenty years in peacetime. If the scale of demand for sheer numbers of soldiers experienced in the First World War was to be repeated, force generation and regeneration in this sense would be nigh on impossible.

The challenges for military leaders in the period to 2030 will be greater than ever. It is worth identifying some now. The compatibility of individuals with and for 'real' military service, is a predisposition and behavioural tendency the Regular Commission Board (RCB) seeks to find in would-be officers, with growing difficulty. More sensitive, less fatalistic attitudinal trends are obvious in the general population as well as the military constituency. A new 'them' and 'us' division differentiates the 'short term' and the 'career' armies within the one British Army. Only one in ten is a 'career' officer or NCO. Ninety per cent of the Army is under the age of thirty.[37]

The 'regimental system' has long been the carrier of the social-anthropological dynamics of military compatibility (which is a variable) and the difference between the short term and the career members within the unit, through the agency of the commanders and leaders. Inducing inclusiveness within a 'range of human relationships', to achieve a high 'quality of human relationships', are other demands on leaders; they too are selection criteria at the RCB. The 'military compatibility' of members combining to produce *Realmilitär* units, another way of saying high quality 'real' soldiers, is not easily achieved when individuals face a characterless monolithic 'military machine'. 'Mutual trust', the currency of 'fighting spirit' belongs to an 'organic', familial organization identified in Tönnies's *Gemeinschaft*[38] of human groupings. This is based on kinship (including that assumed) and status, rather than formal contract.

Further pressures on the British Army of the future to centralise yet remain decentralised,[39] are consequences of the twin recognition of the Revolution in Military Affairs and the more recent Revolution in International Affairs[40] identified by James Gow. Forty years ago there was no 'officer corps' as such. Officers, as in 1881 and before, were to centralise yet remain commissioned into a regiment, not the Army. Now an officer corps exists particularly for those career officers who identify still with their regiments in name, uniform and maybe spirit, but are in truth part of a general staff corps, twice or possibly three times loaned back to their 'own regiment' for command appointments. Whether, in view of the relentless military imperative for joint-service integration, a Joint Service Staff Corps will emerge,[41] one should not be surprised if this were to happen and create a new *caesura* between the leaders and the led.

We are now in the age of the European Rapid Reaction Force. Its 'neo-' derivatives will almost certainly be a European Army, whatever Lord Robertson, the NATO Secretary-General says now in 2001.[42] I find the 'European Security and Defence Identity' difficult to comprehend, except as a statement of algebraic nicety. To what does it add up?

It appears that in military forces of the future, small-group cohesion will become the overriding imperative of how we configure our armed forces. There is a strong likelihood that by 2030 the idea of mixed-nationality military units will have arrived some years earlier, even if nationality becomes a fading concept, with a few trace elements left. Paradoxically regionality may be reasserted, albeit a sort of multi-cultural and multi-ethnic regionality, to provide for necessary small-group cohesion. The likelihood of land-based 'total war' may fade so far, that sub-military gendarmerie units may be the predominant components of 'security power', rather than 'military power', in conducting peace support operations.

The human experience of military service in the decades ahead, both on operations and when 'stood down' – we can hardly envisage the state of peacetime – may produce a continuous state of existential disequilibrium. The only authentic experiences may be those individually recognised and understood, at least partially. The changing nature of what should be a rational, concrete set of circumstances and events shared collectively, may become more elusive and inauthentic than ever. Communicating (in every sense) and acting with other free-thinking agents, may test individuals more than ever before and leadership have to be re-defined for every new contingency.

Group activity, however, is surely the most pervasive of all military imperatives, with the complexity of personal ethical understanding and norms of moral behaviour, needed to achieve extraordinary human tasks, which differentiate operational from day to day activities. It is worth heeding Tolstoy's view of

> "...the primary truth of war: namely that in war the most intelligent units of action are relatively small groups of men, in close physical contact and operationally interdependent, who share, as if by animal magnetism, the same reactions and feelings, whether in the form of resolution or faint-heartedness, of renewed dedication to, or of blind flight from, the demands of their terrible trade."[43]

This conception of soldiering I believe to be the most enduring principle of all.

There is much we do not know about the motivation of soldiers and what can be achieved by military force, bravely used in battle and sparingly used in peace support operations. We have to take account of the extraordinary resilience of the British Army, its tradition for volunteer soldiering, its modern professionalism yet unmilitaristic style. Its people are far superior in spirit than even its weaponry, technology, systems, bureaucracy and all the 'isms of sophisticated military concepts. The future system must integrate and regenerate small groups continuously, while training for the highest competence in both combat and peace support operations. Integrity has two meanings as it did in 1914. Courage and morale are unchanging. The more intensely human the system remains, the more effective it will be – however armies are defined and identified.

That is why, somehow, the decentralised British regimental system will remain in some shape or form, possibly acting as a model for all effective professional armies. Most European armies have long lost the concept of the 'real regiment', the 'total institution', an imperative not only for winning wars and achieving operational tasks, but for unit survival. Intuitively the corporate wisdom of the British Army still appears to induce belief in 'the regiment'. Neo, quasi, virtual, existential, these prefixes are quizzical terms handy for academics. The 'real' regiment, as likely as not, is the one you joined at the start of your service. Full it was of real live human beings, with whom you mucked along. Much more real they were too, than any digitised, virtuality-inducing ephemera you happened to operate along the way. Who would die for an agency, a low level budget or the mother of all computer systems?

NOTES

1. Hackett, General Sir John. *The Profession of Arms.* Sidgwick and Jackson, 1983, p.224.
2. Chapple, Field Marshal Sir John. Interview in *Soldier* Magazine, 11 December 1989.
3. Anonymous officer, 'Bucephalus'. 'Some thoughts in the Regimental System' in *British Army Review*, No.91, April 1989, p.45.
4. Beevor, Antony. *Inside the British Army.* Chatto and Windus, 1990, p.234.
5. Dietz, Peter. *The Last of the Regiments, Their Rise and Fall*, Brassey's, 1990, p.228. Von Zugbach R.G.L. Power and Prestige in the British Army. Gower, 1988.
6. Paskell, Colonel C. W. *An Analysis of the British Army Regimental System.* MDA Thesis, Royal Military College of Science/Cranfield University, 1994, p.29.
7. Ministry of Defence (Army). *Design for Military Operations. The British Military Doctrine.* Army Code 71451, 1989 and 1996.
8. Goffman, Erving. 'The characteristics of Total Institutions' in Etzioni Amitai (ed.) *A Sociology and Reader on Complex Organizations.* Holt, Rinehart and Winston, 1961.
9. 'Mortification processes', for the 1881 regiment, included indoctrination, and imposed discipline. Goffman recognises five categories of such incorporations of persons. They are,

    1. 'homes for the...incapable and harmless;
    2. places...to care...for the incapable...and threat to the community,...
    3. institutions...to protect the community...[from] intentional danger...
    4. institutions purportedly established to better pursue some technical task and justifying themselves only on these instrumental grounds,...
    5. establishments designed...as retreats.' (pp.315–324.)

    Such total institutions include orphanages, mental asylums, gaols and monasteries. In Goffman's fourth category, 'established to better pursue some technical task', he lists as examples 'army barracks, ships, boarding schools, work camps, colonial compounds...' (p.313).

10. Ibid. p.313
11. Baynes, Sir John. *Morale. A Study of Men and Courage.* Cassell, 1967. While more specific in contents, in my view it is as important a book as Lord Moran's better known, *The Anatomy of Courage.* Constable, 1945.
12. Ibid. pp.253–254.
13. Ibid. pp.253.
14. Ibid. pp.100–101.
15. Ministry of Defence (Army). *Soldiering. The Military Covenant.* Army

Doctrine Publication, No 5, Army Code 71642, 2000. Subsidiary documents are entitled *Values and Standards of the British Army for the Army.*

16. I am borrowing the word *Realmilitär* as a parallel expression to *Realpolitik,* as an ontological notion of 'real' soldiering, the obverse of the metaphysical 'notion' of soldiering. Real soldiering, however, in the British tradition, has strong elements of anti-militarism. While German officers were militaristic to a fault in the first half of the twentieth century, British officers retained common sense and the spirit of sportsmanship

17. Quoted in Mileham, Patrick. *Difficulties Be Damned!* Fleur de Lys publishing, 2000, p.125. Lieutenant-Colonel Wilfrith Elstob's VC citation is singled out for inclusion in the Sandhurst anthology *Serve to Lead.*

18. Extract from Army Training Memorandum No. 38, February 1941, quoted in Ministry of Defence (Army) *Training,* Army Doctrine Publication, Volume 4, pp.2–9.

19. Harvey, A. D. *Collision of Empires: Britain in Three World Wars 1793–1945.* London, Pimlico 1992, pp.557 and 560.

20. Ibid. p.557.

21. Barnett, Correlli. *Britain and Her Army 1509–1970.* London, Pelican Books, 1974, p.488.

22. 'The maintenance of regimental integrity in the Foot Guards is of paramount importance'. This statement can be found on page 2 A-2, Annex A to chapter 2 of *Queen's Regulations for the Army.*

23. Curtis, Nicky. *Faith and Duty,* André Deutsch, 1998, pp.92–100, refers to Northern Ireland in the 1970s. The concept of the 'strategic corporal' is widely discussed in peace support operations in the 1990s. See various references in Mileham, Patrick and Willett, Lee (eds.), *Military Ethics for the Expeditionary Era.* Royal Institute of International Affairs, 2001.

24. Hockey, John. *Squaddies. Portrait of a Sub-Culture.* University of Exeter Press, 1986, p.72.

25. Kirke, Charles. 'A Model for the Analysis of Fighting Spirit in the British Army', in Strachan, Hew (ed.) *The British Army, Manpower and Society into the Twentieth Century.* London and Portland, OR, Frank Cass, 2000, pp.227–241.

26. Hables Gray, Chris. *Postmodern War.* London, Routledge, 1997, p.200.

27. Simpkin, Richard. *Race to the Swift.* Brassey's, 1985.

28. Ministry of Defence (Army). *Design for Military Operations. The British Military Doctrine.* Army Code 71451, 1989, p.41.

29. Ibid. p.3.

30. 'We must stop doing philosophy until we get our psychology straight', is the advice of Roger Crisp and Michael Slote in *Virtue Ethics.* Oxford University Press, 1997, p.2.

31. Ministry of Defence (Army). *Soldiering. The Military Covenant.* Army Doctrine Publication, No 5., Army Code 71642, 2000. p.3–1.

32. Ibid. p.3–2.

33. Ibid. pp.3–11 and 3–12.

34. Ibid. p.1–1.

35. Quoted in Gallie, W.B. *Philosophers of Peace and War.* Cambridge University Press, 1978, p.111.

36. Ministry of Defence (Army). *Design for Military Operations. The British Military Doctrine.* Army Code 71451, 1989, pp.3–3, states that 'all British soldiers have the capability for leadership and may be called upon to display it on operations'.

37. Army spokesman quoted in *The Times, 27 February 1997.*

38. Tönnies, Ferdinand. *Community and Association.* Michigan University Press, (1877) 1957.

39. Brigadier Richard Applegate writes of the future Army being 'based on a modular approach'. 'Towards the Future Army' in *The Nature of Future Conflict:Implications for Force Developments*, Strategic and Combat Studies Institute, Occasional Paper Number 36, 1998, p.87.
40. Gow, James. 'A Revolution in International Affairs – Governance, Justice and War', in *International Relations*, Vol.15, No.1, April 2000, p.1.
41. Granville-Chapman, Lieutenant General Sir Timothy. 'Strands in the Nature of Future Conflict and Implication for the British Army' in *Seaford House Papers*, Royal College of Defence Studies, 1993, p.30.
42. 'There is, and will be, no single European Army' stated Lord Robertson at the Royal United Services Institute Medal presentation, 1 March 2001.
43. Gallie, op. cit. p.104.

7

The Volunteers

PETER CADDICK-ADAMS

Cranfield University, Royal Military College of Science

The aim of this chapter is to examine the links between the various uniformed volunteer organisations, and suggest methods of greater cooperation for the future. In considering the voluntary organisations that have a public role and wear uniform to perform it, this chapter interprets the idea of the 'volunteer' in the widest possible sense. There are the obvious military services that shadow their Regular counterparts – the 4,000-strong Royal Naval Reserve, the 1,000 members of the Royal Marine Reserve, some 42,000 men and women of the Territorial Army and 2,500 in the Royal Auxiliary Air Force – who all receive payment for the time they serve and have suffered substantial cuts to their numbers in the last decade.[1]

Those who serve in the reserve military forces frequently manage two careers (and two incomes), carving a second, parallel career from their service, progressing in skill and responsibility. In a sense one would hesitate to designate the Regular military as 'professionals', as many part-timers would regard their contribution as professional, as well. Active service on operations, such as Bosnia or Kosovo, suggests that the military reserves are often every bit as professional as their regular counterparts, and sometimes impossible to tell apart.

The chapter also includes another set of uniformed voluntary organisations, who outnumber the reserve military; it is no accident that many of them are seen on Remembrance Sunday, for they have sprung from the wartime needs of the nation, or pre-conflict nervousness. They include 4,500 RNLI sailors and mechanics that crew the nation's lifeboats, 15,000 Special Constables across the country, the Retained Fire Service (the nation's part-time Firefighters who crew 60 per cent of fire engines) numbering

15,000 men and women, the 80,000 volunteers of the British Red Cross, and the 82,000 members of the St John's Ambulance Brigade. All of these perform a valuable service, often hazardous, and frequently while holding down a full-time job. Some are paid for their time, like the military reserves and Retained Firefighters, but many, like the Special Constables, perform their public duties without remuneration or reward. Then there is the WRVS, who at 98,000 volunteers (of whom 15 per cent are men) is Britain's largest practical volunteering organisation.[2] These organisations alone total 345,000, or over one per cent of the available adult population of the UK.[3]

There are many other uniformed organisations that would merit inclusion, but have been omitted on grounds of size, or ignorance. No slur is intended on their activities, and their inclusion will only strengthen the observations made in this chapter. Apart from some obvious similarities of a requirement to wear some form of uniform, all these bodies promote the concept of 'good citizenship', a popular notion with many Western governments as the 21st century dawns. For the purposes of this study, the uniformed cadet movements, which may feed legions of recruits into these organisations, or other uniformed youth movements such as the Boy's Brigade, Church Lad's Brigade, Scouts or Guides, have been excluded. While it can be argued that they perform the essential function of educating future generations of volunteers, they do not directly contribute to the nation in the way that the more mature, adult organisations do.

HISTORY

Many of the United Kingdom's uniformed volunteer organisations reach back over a century and find their origin in the civic-minded Victorian era, or earlier. The Special Constables, Retained Fire Service, Rifle Volunteers and Yeomanry Cavalry originated in the late 18th century and early 19th century. Indeed there is a strong British tradition of relying on part-time volunteers to get the job done, rather than full-timers – the British repugnance for compulsory military service is a good illustration of this compared to, until recently, the Continental European norm of conscription for all.

A by-product of the industrial revolution was the creation of vast urban sprawls, which fostered a discontented, organised labouring class. As many of the early uniformed volunteers were used to control the growing pains of 19th century urban Britain, there, one suspects, remains a traditional and understandable socialist and trades union suspicion of any large group in uniform. The Yeomanry charged Mancunians in the Peterloo Massacre of 1819, the Territorial Army were called out to police the Coal Strike in 1922 and enrolled as Special Constables in the General Strike of 1926, while Special Constables served throughout the Miners' Strike of 1983–4. The forerunners of the TA – the county volunteer militias and Yeomanry – were frequently called out to keep public order in mid-Victorian Britain, but gradually gave way to regular police forces and special constables.

The latter were established in 1831 by the Special Constables Act, which defined what constituted a Special Constable and his powers. It authorised Justices of the Peace to nominate and appoint as many Special Constables as they thought fit from among the householders and other persons residing in the locality, when they considered there were too few ordinary police officers to preserve peace and protect inhabitants and their property. The Women's Voluntary Service, WVS (later WRVS), was formed in the war-scare era of 1938 to help with evacuation, emergency feeding, clothing and providing general care and support to the community. Today, the service continues to provide practical care and support where it is needed in local hospitals, communities and emergencies, operating in every county, region, major town and city in England, Scotland and Wales.

If there is a lingering working class suspicion of the uniformed volunteer organisations, there is also a danger that they may seem out of step with multi-cultural 21st century Britain – they may appear as white, middle class, Christian organisations, descendants of the Lady of the Manor distributing *largesse*. This cultural 'chasm' is understandable, as the voluntary sector grew from, or flourished in, wartime Britain. Somehow in peacetime the needs of the community, though just as pressing, seem to be someone else's problem, and the inclination to contribute time and skill is increasingly seen as old-fashioned. Modern life seems to suggest so many exciting alternatives to donning a uniform, patrolling the streets and looking for people to help. For the 3 million members of the ethnic minority communities,[4] it is difficult to see how the voluntary services appeal at all. With no folk memory of a need for them, or service with them, the Black or Asian teenager of today must surely struggle with the notion of voluntary service in uniformed organisations which barely recruit any ethnic minorities into their Regular ranks.

The uniforms, while off-putting to some, are important nevertheless. They arguably establish credibility and authority when it is needed and ensure a measure of discipline within the ranks – an important consideration when lives are at stake. Uniforms also hint at uniformity – a common (implicitly efficient) approach to training, and suggest a high standard of individual expertise. Unfortunately, uniforms can also focus hostility from a crowd. Culturally, it is important to get the balance of uniforms in society right. Too many uniforms can lead to the appearance of a police state, a sort of quasi-Third Reich, where even the postmen had ranks and medals. The United Kingdom is not a military society, though some argue that by 1900 Britain was a militaristic society. With so many volunteer youth organisations in late-Victorian Britain, certainly one scholar argues that as many as one in four British males had worn a uniform in some organisation or other, prior to their eighteenth birthday.[5] Today, long after the demise of National Service (abolished in 1960), that would be unacceptable.

Perhaps the balance is shifting too far away from uniformed organisations. Although an increasing number of people in a variety of occupations wear uniforms – witness the dubious growth of the private security industry – they rarely carry status or rank in the way of the military. The United Kingdom has become so demilitarised that few in the population could recognise rank when confronted with it, or confidently tell a Major General from an AA patrolman. A visit to Italy or France (both of whom suffered a Fascist occupation, rife with repressive, uniform-wearing thugs) nevertheless reveals a wider variety of uniforms routinely worn on the streets, with no perceptible damage to the fabric of society.

RECRUITMENT AND RETENTION

Every uniformed volunteer organisation, from the Territorial Army to the Red Cross, reports that there is a real struggle both to retain adequate numbers of trained personnel, and to attract new recruits and keep them. The National Council of the St John's Ambulance Brigade held a 'crisis conference' in September 2000 to address this very issue. Each organisation searches its soul for the errors they are making in advertising, recruitment or training, but the trend is national, and afflicts all. This is probably no fault of theirs, but today there are so many other ways of spending one's leisure time. There has never been so much 'quality time', yet ironically, it has never been so valuable as today. Better salary packages mean more money to spend on holidays, sport and hobbies. Lifestyle is promoted via every media, creating ever-higher personal expectations, which can only eat into the spare time that was traditionally set aside to spend on voluntary activities.

It is not just a question of money, for the military reserves, lifeboatmen and Retained Firefighters are paid for their time but still have the same problems as the remainder who are not. Bizarrely, the Special Constabulary (unfairly labeled 'Hobby Bobbies' by their Regular counterparts) remain unpaid for their time, although the Home Office are reportedly considering adjusting this anomaly.[6]

Yet it would be wrong to think this a new phenomenon. Since their birth in 1908, the Territorials have always had a recruiting problem. Even in the lean years of the 1930s, they ran at a 25–30 per cent wastage rate. Whatever the manpower establishment, the Territorials seem to hover at 10 per cent below. The same is true for many other voluntary organisations. If one accepts that all the voluntary organisations – this is true with the Specials, Retained Firefighters and Red Cross – never attain their establishment, and lose a healthy percentage each year, does this matter? If one of the strategic (and implicit) aims of these organisations is to promote responsible citizenship, then should they not be happy that they are still able to recruit and train our volunteers, even if only for a frustratingly brief period?

Unfortunately, a large leakage of personnel will probably affect the ability of each organisation to perform its role in society, as a disproportionate effort is put into recruitment, retention and training. (This is another reason for excluding the youth movements from this chapter: they only have recruits for a fixed term, until they get too old. They are a mass turnover organisation, yet – against the trend of other voluntary uniformed organisations – survive and flourish.) If instead of trying the shore up these losses, what if they were seen as positive, that keeping someone for only two or three years was regarded as a positive contribution? If it is made easier to enter and leave all these organisations – or transfer between them (which is not easy at present) – volunteers could leave with their head held high. As most actually leave, not because of boredom, but because of either a change of job, marriage, or the arrival of children, they might (if encouraged) return in the future, when their personal circumstances permit.

Some argue that to best serve the society of which they are the fabric, the uniformed volunteer organisations should reflect that society. With the notion of the 'job for life' and the concept of long service in a single company shattered beyond recovery now, where in many professions the sign of personal progress is frequent job changes, trading up company cars, salaries and pension plans, should not the volunteer organisations reflect this to a degree as well, in expecting to keep their people for shorter periods?

If these organisations are all very seriously worried by the challenge of recruitment and retention, what else do or might they have in common? The crossover is wider than one might first think. With the grouping of the emergency services on common sites, the Retained Firefighters and Special Constables have already formed closer links, and worked hand-in-glove with the Territorial Army in the 2000 floods and 2001 Foot and Mouth outbreak. It is often forgotten that the ever-elusive Honourable Artillery Company has long had its own division of Special Constables, as well as infantry and artillery detachments. Clearly the St John's Ambulance, British Red Cross and Royal Army Medical Corps have a great deal of commonality, and the Territorial Royal Military Police have long formally recruited from the regular police forces and the AA. In France, one might be surprised to learn that the Paris Fire Brigade of 7,500 and Marseilles Fire Service of 2,500 are serving regular military personnel, who are posted routinely in and out of these units.

Though it is not the place of this chapter to suggest another role for the army, the roles of the different volunteer organisations have perhaps more in common than they themselves first realise. Take the notion of recruitment, for example. Each uniformed volunteer service makes its own arrangements for recruitment, mostly on a county-by-county basis. The Special Constabulary is particularly bad at this, recruiting and training only on a constabulary basis, with no effort at national supervision. Retained Firefighters are recruited on a station-by-station basis. Yet unit surveys, conducted informally within the Territorial Army, suggest that soldiers had already looked at another uniformed volunteer service before joining the TA, and many end up in another at some stage after leaving the TA. This suggests two things. That recruitment to the volunteer organisations on a nationally coordinated basis is far more effective than on a local basis, and that the best kind of recruit is one already used to wearing a uniform, and used to putting time aside for voluntary service on a regular basis.

Taken to its logical conclusion, one might suggest that the uniformed volunteer organisations recruited together, and were seen as different cards in the same pack. They could swap potential recruits, and point those leaving in the direction of further voluntary service, paid or unpaid. Potentially, this is a powerful argument, for it could minimise the cost of recruiting. This can be demoralisingly extortionate: for example, in 1998, a £2 million recruitment programme for the Special Constabulary resulted in a national net increase of just six Special Constables, partly because the accompanying wastage rate (running at a shocking 20 per cent per annum) greatly exceeded the recruitment rate.[7] Carefully-managed, shared television commercials, or 'One-Stop' Recruitment 'shops' might therefore provide a cost-effective, partial solution to recruitment.

The Reserve Forces were concerned about losing their volunteer forces 'footprint' in local communities, during the recent round of drill hall closures, brought about by the Strategic Defence Review. Perhaps, with shared recruiting, if the concept of voluntary service in a uniformed organisation was considered in a wider context, more could be done formally to redirect redundant Territorials to the Red Cross, or Special Constabulary, for example. The United Kingdom military forces have grown closer together in the last decade, with the adoption of 'Joint' (i.e. tri-service) doctrine, which has led to (in some cases) to tri-service training establishments. This argument takes the tri-service concept further. Such a combined approach by *all* the uniformed voluntary organisations could lead to more inter-organisational training, and might attract some commercial sponsorship, which the voluntary sector so desperately needs.

A good contemporary example of private sector support was the sponsorship by Norwich Union Insurance of the St John's Ambulance Brigade.[8] Norwich Union wanted to reinforce their brand message of 'No One Protects More' and after much research decided to promote First Aid, which was relevant to everybody and would promote goodwill for the company nationally. They sponsored free places on tailor-made St John's Ambulance First Aid courses and funded promotional material inviting viewers to call a hotline number to book on to the courses. Nationally, the project resulted in over 13,000 people receiving free first aid training.

Before the voluntary sector hold up their hands in horror at the thought of jumping into bed with the corporate sector, it is worth recalling that most of the uniformed voluntary organisations sprang from commercial sponsorship in the 18th and 19th centuries. The fire services and some police forces began in this fashion, while many infantry companies of the Territorial Force were overtly sponsored by businesses at its inception on 1 April 1908. In Birmingham, for example, there was a BSA Company and a Mitchell's and Butler's Company – both formations (each about 200-strong) recruited exclusively from a local firm, where the managers were officers, and the foremen, NCOs. Indeed, without commercial sponsorship of urban Territorial units in Edwardian Britain, some authors argue that Territorial Force recruitment would have been a disaster.[9] So the precedents have been set. What price to sponsor a Territorial Army vehicle?

Seeing the military volunteer organisations as part of the same deck of cards as, say, the Retained Firefighters or Red Cross might well help to remove lingering suspicions of uniformed organisations as 'strike-breakers'. Gender and ethnic challenges in recruiting may be easier to manage in a nation-wide, multi-organisational recruiting campaign, too, and the likelihood of employers seeing voluntary service as a threat to the efficiency of their workforce may diminish if, say, the British Red Cross or St John's Ambulance Brigade are perceived to play as important a role in promoting responsibility and good citizenship as the Territorial Army or Special Constabulary. A common approach to recruitment, possibly even some training, might well encourage greater respect and support for the volunteer movement *as a whole*, as well as foster a better understanding of each organisation by their other volunteer contemporaries.

The purpose of this chapter has not been to suggest a uniformed society where all the trains run on time, but rather, to suggest a time when more of society helps to turn the wheels to begin with.

NOTES

1. Establishment figures given in House of Commons Select Committee on Defence, Eighth Report, September 1998, paragraph 264.
2. Figures from the Internet websites of each organisation accessed January–March 2001.
3. According to *Whitaker's Almanack* for 2000, there are approx. 34 million males and females between 16 and 65 (for men) and 60 (for women), out of a population of approximately 57 million.
4. According to the 1991 Census.
5. Blanch, J. 'Nation, Empire and the Birmingham Working Class 1899–1914'. Unpublished PhD thesis, University of Birmingham, October 1975.
6. D. Bamber, 'Pay plans to boost special constables', *The Sunday Telegraph*, 28 January 2001.
7. Tina Orr-Munro, 'A Special Concern', *Police Review*, 1 September 2000, p.16.
8. Sue Adkins, *Cause Related Marketing, Who Cares Wins*. Butterworth Heinemann, 1999.
9. See, for example, Peter Caddick-Adams, *By God They Can Fight*, Shrewsbury 1995, Chapter One.

8

Reassessing Recruiting Strategies for the Armed Services

HEW STRACHAN
University of Glasgow

The British Armed Forces are now very small. The Army needs about 11,000 recruits a year, the Navy less than half that. It is tempting therefore to talk not of recruiting strategies but tactics. Minor adjustments have much larger consequences than would be the case with bigger establishments. Furthermore, the issues are not always susceptible to calculations that are 'purple'. Any attempt to generalise for the three services obscures significant differences, not only between them but also within each of them. Finding naval nurses is different from finding air force pilots, and there can be vacancies in one specialism in one year which are not there in the next.

In many ways, therefore, the logical approach to the issues of recruiting is to go for detail, to engage in an exercise in number-crunching – to show trends over time, to catalogue ages on enlistment, the regional backgrounds of recruits, their sex, their ethnic origins, and their educational attainments. Most service responses do exactly this: they take a specific issue and endeavour to resolve it. But however successful such individual initiatives are, they never seem to resolve the underlying malaise – that, even if the government responded to the services' pleas that they are overstretched by increasing their establishments, they would struggle to fill their ranks. Indeed the 1998 Strategic Defence Review, which increased the regular Army by 3,500, illustrates this very point. Throughout the 1990s the Army regularly said it was 5,000 men under strength. By increasing the target the SDR deepened the Army's recruiting problem rather than resolved it. The Chief of the General Staff told *The Times* on 3 August 1999 that the Army was now short of 6,000 men. And the Army, although in a worse position than the other two services, is not alone. The effect on the RAF of the Strategic Defence Review was neutral and it cut the Royal Navy by 1,400, and yet in 1999 the former did not expect to be fully manned until 2000 and the latter until 2002. In other words there is a gap between the Armed Forces' demand and society's ability to supply. What underpins recruitment, therefore, is the relationship between the Armed Forces and society.

Moreover, recruitment cannot be separated from retention. In 1997 the underlying shortfall in Army recruiting was deemed to be not 5,000 but 15,000 – in other words the failure to enlist was being covered by the improved retention of senior soldiers. But in 1999 Army recruiting was more buoyant: the Chief of the General Staff said that it had risen 12 per cent. But the Army still will not be fully manned in 2004 if it cannot hold on to those it already has. For the Army in particular, recruiting and retention go hand in glove.[1]

The recruiting problem is greater for the Army than for the other two services – partly because its manpower totals are higher, but principally because of the difficulty in relating its common denominator skill, that of the infantry soldier, to any other body of skills. In the long run the revolution in military affairs may prove a palliative: the automated battlefield implies a convergence between the technical skills of civilians and those of servicemen. But there are two reasons for being cautious about any optimism on these grounds. The first is asymmetric warfare. Any troops deployed to face the machetes and small arms of the Indonesian militia in East Timor will need old-fashioned fighting skills, not the technicalities of the 'revolution in military affairs'. Peacekeeping and peace-enforcement are likely to sustain the demand for infantry traditionally defined. And the second concern is that, even if the revolution in military affairs did effect a greater convergence between the workplaces of the Armed Forces and of civilian society, its consequences could well be to deepen the difficulties of retention. The skills of the servicemen would be readily transferable.

At the moment, however, the transferability of skills creates major retention problems in only one area, that of pilots. Elsewhere specialists, including engineers, tend to stay. Ironically, it seems that many of those who leave prematurely are precisely those who have most cause to be apprehensive about their employment prospects outside the service. Their departure is rationalised as a consequence of overstretch, although, as the House of Commons Defence Committee has observed, there is no common understanding what this means.[2] Not all elements of the Armed Forces are under identical strains. Furthermore, boredom and inactivity are far more potent enemies to retention.

Very often overstretch seems to mean little more than increased commitments being met by smaller Armed Forces. In the early 1990s the worry for the services was the loss of strategic focus consequent on the ending of the Cold War. That deficit has now been made good. The Conservative government, beginning in 1993 with Malcolm Rifkind's review, *Front Line First*, adopted some of the rhetoric of a global, interventionist and humanitarian defence policy, but it is Tony Blair's Labour government which has converted it into practice. Ends are declared – whether it is the allocation of a brigade to the UN, or the dispatch of a reinforced Gurkha company to East Timor – which outstrip the means. Thus the oft-quoted statistic of the late 1990s, that 30 per cent of the Army is deployed on operations or returning from them or preparing to depart for them, is revised upwards on an almost daily basis – to 41 per cent according to the Chief of the General Staff in February 1999, and to 80 per cent for the Royal Corps of Signals.[3] But this too begs for definition: when is a deployment an operation?

Operations, particularly when they are conducted with success, are good publicity. The Armed Forces are held in universally high regard by the public. In the past such respect has rarely found reflection in recruitment; the man in the street has been very happy to doff his cap to the profession of arms without any intention of taking the shilling himself. But this seems to be less the case at the beginning of the twenty-first century. At the moment the Army is getting nearly twice as many applicants as it has places, and naval recruiting is charting a similarly upward graph. The worry, however, is that the overstretch which operations generate for small Armed Forces undermines any successes at the recruiting end of the equation by failures of retention. Indeed in the views of some commentators the one has become almost the corollary of the other.

The existence of a gap between the Army's establishment and its actual strength is not new. Consider both a comparatively recent perspective and a longer-term one. In 1988, before the end of the Cold War, the Army was 1.5 per cent below establishment. Furthermore, the age group from which it recruited was forecast to shrink by 20 per cent in the next five years, particularly in the lower social categories from which it drew its soldiers. It set about addressing the problem under the acronym MARILYN (Manpower and Retention in the Lean Years of the Nineties).[4] Then came the end of the Cold War. In 1992 *Options for Change* reduced the Army's establishment from 156,000 to 116,000, and ought to have resolved the difficulty. The fact that it did not suggests that the underlying issues are more fundamental and longer term than a focus on the oscillations of annual rates suggests.

The mismatch between demand and supply would have been familiar in 1899. On the eve of the Boer War, then as now, the Armed Forces were held in high popular regard but drew on only a very small proportion of society for their members. Those who were unemployed or paid only by the day were much more likely to enlist in the Army than those with skills or in white-collar jobs. The fact that most of its men came from the slums of industrial England meant that medical rejection rates were high. Throughout the nineteenth century Britain had almost as small an Army as today's but even so it struggled to fill its ranks.

The sense that recruiting in Britain is not inherently difficult relies on a medium-term memory, and derives from the experience of conscription in 1916–18 and 1939–60. The effect of compulsory military service was to unite the Armed Forces and society, to create a true nation in arms, and to give every British family a sense of belonging to, and association and participation with, the services. During the Second World War Britain was genuinely the offshore aircraft carrier of Europe; none of its major cities was far from the sea, and the Battle of the Atlantic emphasised the primacy of its maritime heritage in national survival; the regimental system, which amazingly was extended and adapted to the needs of a mass Army, broke the Army into a network of regional loyalties.

There were two further consequences inherent in major

European war. First, the acceptance of military service was unequivocal. The nation existed to fight, and the Armed Forces' mission was at bottom defensive. Second, the effect was not just to universalise the experience of military service but also to militarise society. The traditions of individualism and liberalism, which are inherently inimical to the communal ethos of the armed services, are a legacy of Victorian Britain; the two world wars moderated them, overlaying them with collectivism. War caused civilian society to embrace many of the virtues close to the hearts of services.

Crucially, however, conscription was seen as a temporary wartime phenomenon, an attitude not moderated by its persistence until 1960. Unlike France or many of the other countries of continental Europe, Britain has no tradition of military service as a corollary of citizenship or of political rights. Since conscription's abolition, the separateness of the Armed Forces from society, what can be seen as the 'normal' condition of Britain, has reasserted itself. In civilian life, individualism has regained its primacy, whereas the Armed Forces have continued to stress the ethos of collective loyalty. Significantly the Armed Forces' 'right' to be different has become even more pressing; it is now defined as a 'need'. Furthermore this cultural divergence is deepening, a trend which can be quantified in terms which have immediate implications for recruiting. In 1997, 20 per cent of those aged 35–45 had direct links with individuals with military backgrounds; the same was true for only 7 per cent of those aged 16–24.[5]

The situation today does, therefore, bear more than a passing comparison with that of a century ago. Moreover, it does so for reasons that are more profound than those of the Armed Forces' structure. In 1899 the immediate function of the Army was to police the empire. Then, as now, it was not national self-defence. Much colonial warfare was vicious and, at least for those on the receiving end, total. But from the perspective of London, its thrust was limited, and its conduct restrained. Today the Armed Forces' tasks are humanitarian and the responsibilities which Britain assumes are those of the international community rather than of the individual nation state. These are not matters of national survival; the forces are not defending home, hearth and loved ones. The job is an honourable one, but it is also less immediate.

It creates two paradoxes for the business of recruiting. First the mission of the Armed Forces today is the maintenance of peace rather than the conduct of war. Soldiers are portrayed as social workers, counsellors, nurses and aid workers – indeed almost everything except warriors. But the young man or woman who wants to be a psychotherapist or a doctor will not see the Armed Forces as a logical career. Those who want to join the Army want to fight; they may even want to kill. The Armed Forces can attract psychopaths but they do not like them, or at least not in the current operational environment, that of peacekeeping rather than of war.

Second the parental perception of the military career is that it is one in which the risks are high. We are constantly told that a major restraint on the western democracies' use of force is the self-imposed one of the fear of casualties. But Britain's recent experience of combat does not endorse this perception. Both the Falklands and the Gulf were short, sharp wars with comparatively low death rates. Britain has just taken part in a war in Kosovo in which it suffered two fatalities. This is among a group of men and women whose readiness to take risks is presumably higher than that of society as a whole; probably more would have died or been injured in road traffic accidents or in pub brawls if they had been at home than if they had been in the Balkans. That was certainly *Time* magazine's conclusion with regard to the US Army's deployment in the Gulf.[6]

Peacekeeping, Christopher Coker has gone on to argue, may be as dangerous as war. But another way of looking at this is to say that war in the twenty-first century is not actually as dangerous as the collective European memory of the Somme or Stalingrad suggests it ought to be. If this is the case, it is crucial to Britain's current systems of recruitment, for at least outwardly they are based on a contradiction.

Their tempo is geared to the maintenance of Armed Forces for low-intensity operations; they effectively assume minimal or no combat casualties. The ability to conscript was repealed in 1977; released regulars have effectively no ongoing reserve training liability; the capacity for rapid and sizeable expansion

105

of the forces is limited, and was reduced by the Strategic Defence Review's handling of the Territorial Army. And yet that same review took as its gold standard the capacity to conduct high intensity operations. Major war would require a very different system of procuring manpower.[7] In 1991 Patrick Cordingley memorably told the press that, once ground fighting got under way, he anticipated casualties in his brigade of up to 15 per cent per day.[8] Presumably, no one was happier than he that he was proved wrong, but what he said was a wholly realistic assessment based on the serious study of major war. He was right in theory, but it is a theory of which we seem almost entirely to have lost sight. The most worrying aspect of all in the current size of Britain's Armed Forces is their inability to renew themselves or to expand; effectively we have a one-shot capability.

High intensity warfare in the past has required a mass conscript Army to conduct it, not a long-service small professional force. The latter is the instrument for what are today called constabulary or gendarmerie operations, and what in the nineteenth century were the tasks of empire and internal order. There is nothing new in a small professional force taking major war as the standard to which it aspires, but in doing so it has to recognise that it is a cadre, not the instrument for conducting that war. It took Britain until 1916 to put the bulk of a mass Army into France in the First World War, and until 1944 to do the same in the Second World War.

Britain's Armed Forces today make a virtue of professionalism to the point of romanticisation. General Sir Mike Jackson is not a romantic, and when commanding in the Balkans he said that regulars, reservists and conscripts had all achieved an acceptable level of interoperability in KFOR.[9] But for many of his British colleagues the regular Army is the only way. The ethos of professionalism is a key component in the divergence between Armed Forces and civilian society. In the Royal Navy it may even be based in reality, as it can claim to be a long-service body. The average time spent in the Navy is 14 years; in practice most of those who stay after nine years do so for at least 22. In the Army the average period in uniform is four years. Its cumulative experience of operations is much more limited than its reputation suggests: 65 per cent of those who served in the Gulf had left by 1999.[10]

Such averaging is of course misleading. Those with positions of responsibility and seniority do have the qualities, and qualifications, of professionalism and experience. But beneath them is a second tier, a short-service Army whose time in uniform may be little more than that of the conscript in the days of national service.[11]

The Armed Forces sell themselves as a career, a strong point when so many civilian jobs, even if providing continuity of location and better short-term salaries, seem to carry higher risks of redundancy. And yet most of those who join the Army, if not the Royal Navy, do not stay.

Attention to this issue tends to focus on the Armed Forces' comparability with civilian society. If service men and women leave early it is said to be because the services are too different from civilian life. Bullying, brutalism and home sickness – the press suggests that these are the lot of the recruit, and the 1999 television series on recruit training did little to soften that image. After overcoming the strains of initiation, servicemen become vulnerable to different demands, those of spouses and children, and their need for stability and continuity. The Ministry of Defence has responded with an employment practice that tries at least outwardly to align the Armed Forces with society, and to foster the integration of the two. This worries many soldiers, who fear an erosion of combat capability as a consequence.

But there is another effect which has been less remarked upon. It also removes the perks of the job, and so erodes the distinctiveness and corporate loyalty of the profession. The process began with the withdrawal from east of Suez. When in the 1970s the services came home from empire, they lost marriage allowances. Servicemen and women began having to pay a more realistic price for quarters and messing. The effects should not be exaggerated, because in reality all the facilities still represent amazingly good value in the context of the wider market, and because pay scales were adjusted to incorporate the benefits in kind which had been lost. But the effect is a weakening in the links of the wider military community at just that point in time when they need reinforcement.

In the nineteenth century the regiment was the soldier's home in a way that was paternalist and self-contained; it achieved it by regulations and conventions with regard to marriage, mess life and children's upbringing which we would now regard as unacceptable intrusions into personal liberty. But the result, a commitment to the services not only as a career but also as a way of life, is precisely what the Ministry of Defence should be seeking to reinforce.

The Navy may provide some pointers here. If prolonged absences and consequent marital strain were the key issues in retention, then its track record in this respect should be far worse than that of the Army. The fact that it is not suggests that there may be institutional responses which work, and that may rest on the recognition of the differences, not the similarities, between a naval career and most civilian employments.

The one substantive recommendation of the Strategic Defence Review in regard to its 'Policy for People', the promise of a full educational programme based on NVQs, however well intentioned, encapsulates these dilemmas.[12] The qualifications are civilian not military, they prepare servicemen for life out of uniform not in it, and they affirm that the services are at best only half a career.

The idea that armed services are schools for the nation – a tradition into which the NVQ track fits – is a familiar one. By imparting qualifications and skills to those who do not possess them and so fitting servicemen to be more productive and better disciplined members of the wider community after their discharge, the forces justify their roles in society. It was an argument cited by both the last two commanders-in-chief of the British Army, Wolseley and Roberts. But its fullest development was probably in Tsarist Russia, where it was used by reformers to rationalise the shift from a long-service Army with a smaller recruiting base to a short-service Army with a much greater recruiting base.[13] In other words it was the argument of those seeking the integration of the Armed Forces and society in the age of the mass, conscript Army, not of a recruiting strategy for Armed Forces that see themselves as long service and professional. If the forces attract recruits on the grounds that they want a career, and if that is what the services wish them to pursue, then that is what must be delivered.

Despite the ageism which now afflicts British employment practices, the cult of youth over experience, even of modism over wisdom, most people in the workforce anticipate employment until the age of 60 or even 65, not 40 or 45 – or even less. But that is the culture the services now generate. Infantry combat may be a young man's vocation, but the teeth arms are only a small proportion of the total Ministry of Defence workforce. The revolution in military affairs should favour the extension of careers. And yet many of the careers are no longer there because they have been civilianised. The passing to outside contractors of tasks that used to be done in-house is reducing the opportunities for the sustained employment of those whose skills and energies are no longer best suited to flying fast jets or negotiating assault courses. In seeing themselves as professions, the forces must also offer full careers.

In doing so, the Ministry of Defence needs to refurbish its reputation as an employer. Its definition of service life as only half a career is confirmed by its public reputation for shoddiness in dealing with those disabled in its service. Both post-traumatic stress disorder and Gulf War syndrome may well owe as much to auto-suggestion as to objective circumstances. But the problems are real enough for those who suffer them, and the fact that they do so is connected to their choice of career. By being constructive rather than defensive, pro-active rather than reactive, the ministry could go a long way towards affirming what its uniformed members instinctively feel – that once you have entered the service you belong in some senses for life, that a commitment by the individual to the institution involves a reciprocal obligation on the part of the institution itself. Disgruntled veterans are poor publicity.

In 1998, 25 per cent of Britain's homeless were reported to be ex-servicemen.[14] At one level this affirms the wisdom of the Ministry of Defence's current strategy: the gap between the Armed Forces and society needs to be closed so that the move from one to another – whether it is enlisting or leaving – can be accomplished with less pain. But another conclusion would point in the opposite direction. The gap is too great to be bridged. We should confront the reality, that buoyant recruiting and retention may be so difficult in our affluent, liberal society that the mechanisms of voluntary enlistment are insufficient.

With no institutionalised tradition of conscription, Britain has had to use other methods to supplement its manpower. The first has been the employment of mercenaries. Europeans, Swiss and Germans, were recruited as recently as the Crimean War. Britain still uses Irishmen. The second has been the use of colonial troops. An exiguous British Army held a global empire because local regiments did the local policing. The Indian Army was the most obvious but not the only example. And in European warfare in the twentieth century the white dominions made major contributions. Over 70 per cent of those in the 8th Army in North Africa in October 1941 came from the empire.[15]

The Gurkhas are the surviving embodiment of both traditions. They are held in deep affection and high esteem in Britain, and yet they have been cut. Thanks to Machiavelli, mercenaries have had a bad press; they fight because war is a trade not a cause, and it is suggested that therefore their loyalties are suspect. But the sort of conflict which we are currently confronting is entirely appropriate to warriors who sell their skills. We want men who know how to fire rifles and have fieldcraft, not those who want NVQs which will get them civilian jobs as lorry drivers or plumbers. We plan to deploy them in theatres where there is no direct issue of national security, but where the interests at stake are those of the international community. It may be a manifestation of our national decadence to get others to do our fighting for us, but we should be recruiting more Gurkhas – and more Irishmen – not fewer.

If this is deemed politically incorrect, then we have no alternative but to resolve the paradox with which current policy has encumbered itself. The Ministry of Defence endorses the Armed Forces' right to be different and yet tries to integrate the services and civil society. It condones homophobia and yet combats racism. The contradictions are more than implicit. The forces probably cannot continue to have it both ways if they are to recruit exclusively, successfully and consistently in British society.

In the nineteenth century, Britain drew its sailors and, above all, its soldiers from the lower ends of the social spectrum. That is still the case. The Army may have almost twice as many recruits as vacancies, but that surplus is soon whittled away by its own selection procedures. Rejection rates on medical grounds in 1997–98 ran at about 40 per cent, a level not very different from that of a century ago.[16] Educational levels among potential infantrymen are also low. Of those who are accepted, the drop-out rate is greatest in the infantry, the arm with the lowest demands in terms of existing qualifications and with the least likelihood of imparting transferable skills. While those going into the technical arms move on to the specialisms of their chosen branch after completing the common infantry syllabus in one of the Army's five training regiments, the infantry go to Catterick for a course that is yet tougher. About 25 per cent drop out. The infantry's demands, of physique, character, and resilience, therefore create their own problems in a recruiting pool that is made up of a cohort that is in general immature, homesick, and ill prepared for the demands that their chosen career thrusts upon them.

But the problem is therefore also on the supply side. In 1899 the working class – if by that we mean those who earnt their livings by manual labour – constituted roughly 80 per cent of those in employment. Today it may be at most 40 per cent, and it is falling. The pool from which the infantry has traditionally drawn is contracting. And yet it has difficulty in fishing elsewhere.

Ethnic minorities make up 7 per cent of the United Kingdom's population, but in 1997 constituted only 0.8 per cent of the Navy and 1.4 per cent of the Army. The figure is rising: the Army achieved the target of 2 per cent in 1998 and the Navy's doubled to 1.5 per cent. But neither service enlisted its 1999 target of 3 per cent.[17] Women are only eligible for 70 per cent of the Army's jobs; until 2000 homosexuals (who admittedly account for only 6.1 per cent of the country's male population and 3.4 per cent of its female[18]) for none. Moreover, the discovery of homosexuality in servicemen led to their discharge, and, until recently, was at least one element, if not a major one, in the retention figures.

For some areas of the UK one or the other of the services seems barely to exist. The Royal Navy recruits disproportionately in the south, and especially close to Portsmouth. Army recruiting flourishes in the north-east of England, but many of its training facilities are in the south, so

111

exacerbating rather than easing the homesickness of late teenagers. Scottish recruiting has always been much more sticky than the public adulation of all things Highland has suggested, but it still accounts for 13 per cent of the total, and military service has been a key component in the forging of a national identity – developed, significantly, within the Union and not outside it. Wales seems barely to figure in any service's calculations. The Ministry of Defence, with its roots in Whitehall, can seem blind to regional loyalties. It makes sense, in the interests of defence policy as a whole, to play up to the aspirations of local identities, not ride roughshod over them.

The key issue, however, is the attitude of the middle class, broadly defined. This is where most British citizens now place themselves. Those who do so, however, will also tend to regard either themselves or their progeny as potential officers. Because all three services have an officer-entry system, gaining a commision via the ranks is perceived to be the exception rather than the rule. And yet if the Armed Forces are truly a profession and a career, the path from non-commissioned service to commissioned needs to be broader and wider.

The services are hesitant about adopting the police as a model. Graduates have not entered the police in the numbers which that service might have hoped. A common entry point may therefore be a deterrent to middle-class enlistment. But if the armed services draw back from the police model, then they must be under even greater pressure to identify earlier those who have entered the ranks who have the potential to be commissioned. The management of the officer/other rank interface is crucial if the services are to be careers of first choice for the offspring of today's middle managers and white-collar workers.

The Royal Navy and the Royal Air Force have been more flexible in this regard. Arguably both from their very inception have been skills-centred services – flying and navigation were paths to promotion. Until recently, however, the Army drew its senior ranks disproportionately from the teeth arms, and those with technical skills, like the Royal Electrical and Mechanical Engineers and Royal Corps of Transport, were unlikely to find their way to the Army Board.

Recent evidence suggests this is changing, and that Eric Joyce was wrong to say that it was not. But the success of his Fabian Society pamphlet points nonetheless to a powerful perception, which it will take years to modify.[19]

The entry roots for those who harbour long-term ambitions in the services may very well be the cadets, the Combined Cadet Forces, the Officers' Training Corps and to a lesser extent the adult reserves. These organisations now justify their existences above all as links between the Armed Forces and society. But, in an age where everything must be quantified, they can also provide direct evidence of their role through their success in recruiting.

For the Army the most exciting development in this respect is the establishment of the Army Foundation College at Harrogate, whose first intake of 315 passed out in 1999. It makes up for the loss of the Junior Leaders, and it bypasses many of the difficulties generated by the Army training regiments. Moreover, by taking school-leavers at 16 (not at 17), it removes the need which previously existed for the motivated and ambitious to fill in a year before entering the Army. The obvious threat to this device is external. It is at odds with the UN declaration on the rights of the child, which defines anybody under the age of eighteen as a child soldier, and forbids their operational deployment. Moreover, the determination to bind the junior soldier to a five-year commitment may be at odds with current civilian employment practices.[20]

But, ironically, the real challenge for the Army will not be how it handles these outside – and more public – challenges, but how it addresses the internal opportunities. The future progress of those who have passed through the Army Foundation College – and ultimately the number who go on to become officers – will be the real test of whether the Army has now plugged the middle-management gap. In the past those who went from the Junior Leaders to commissions did so at an age where their promotion prospects were limited and were likely to remain confined to technical arms.

Thinking strategically about recruiting opens up two lines of thought. One is predicated on a recognition that the Armed Forces and society are divided, that actually armies do not reflect their parent societies, and that societies do not always get the armies they deserve. This enshrines the right to be different. On this basis, the Ministry of Defence should either think about conscription, which it will not, or should make a greater virtue of professionalism in career terms, which is unlikely. The second line of thought follows from that assumption and argues that, if the services are to avoid a continuing sense of crisis, that if they are to have the luxury of selecting those they want, then they must actually do more to integrate themselves with society. This may affront those concerned about 'the right to be different' but compromise might be the precondition for buying into the skills, literacy, motivation, and physical and mental health of those social groups from which the services would most like to draw.

NOTES

This chapter is a revised version of a paper presented at a conference on recruiting and retention organised by the Royal United Services Institute for Defence Studies on 22 September 1999.

1. *The Times*, 3 August 1999 and 4 August 1999; also *Economist*, 17 July 1999; *The Herald* (Glasgow), 23 July 1999 and 12 October 1999.
2. House of Commons Defence Committee, 8th Report, session 1997-8, *Strategic Defence Review*, HC 138–1; oral presentation of report by Bruce George, MP, to Royal United Services Institute for Defence Studies.
3. Lecture to Royal United Services Institute for Defence Studies, 17 February 1999; report in *The Times*, 18 February 1999.
4. *The Times*, 3 November 1988.
5. Hew Strachan (ed.), *The British Army, Manpower and Society into the Twenty-First Century*, London and Portland, OR: Frank Cass, 2000, p.xv.
6. Christopher Coker, 'Post-Modern War', *RUSI Journal*, Vol.143, No.3, June 1998, p.8.
7. General Sir Roger Wheeler, 'The British Army after the SDR: Peacemakers know that Britain will deliver', *RUSI Journal*, Vol.144, No.2, April/May 1999, p.5.
8. *The Times*, 30 November 1990.
9. See also, Cm. 4724, Ministry of Defence, *Kosovo: Lessons from the Crisis*, 8.16
10. A finding of those surveying veterans in relation to Gulf War-related illness, according to Simon Wessely.
11. A point made by Patrick Mileham: see Strachan, *British Army*, p.xxi.
12. Cm. 3899, *Strategic Defence Review*, Stationery Office, July 1998, pp.31–6, and supporting essay 9–1.
13. John Bushnell, 'Peasants in Uniform: the Tsarist Army as Peasant Society', *Journal of Social History*, Vol. 13, 1980, pp.565–76.
14. *The Times*, 8 April 1998.
15. David French, *The British Way in Warfare 1688–2000*, London: Unwin Hyman 1990, p.198.
16. Alan Hawley, 'People not personnel: the human dimension of fighting power', in Strachan, *British Army*, pp 214–16; also p.xv.
17. Cm. 3999, *Strategic Defence Review*, Stationery Office, July 1998, supporting essay 9–1, para.41.

18. Report of the Homosexuality Policy Assessment Team, Ministry of Defence, 1996, p.29.
19. Eric Joyce, 'Arms and the Man – Renewing the Armed Services', *Labour in Action*, Fabian Society Discussion Paper 37, 1997; Reggie von Zugbach de Sugg and Mohammed Ishaq, 'Officer Recruitment and the Decline in Social Eliteness in the Senior Ranks of the British Army', in Strachan, *British Army.*
20. *The Times*, 14 and 16 January 1998, 19 June 1998, 19 October 1999; *Guardian*, 15 January 1998; *Child soldiers: criminals or victims?* Amnesty International report, IOR 50/002/2000, December 2000.

9

Portfolio Careers. The Answer to the Royal Navy's Officer Recruitment and Retention Problems?

JERRY PLANT
Royal Navy

INTRODUCTION

The concept of a 'job for life' has become increasingly outmoded and employees have reacted by taking a far more active role in developing their own careers. Discussion of the 'portfolio career'[1] and 'Me PLC'[2] is indicative of a seismic shift in work culture that has altered the employment landscape. The Armed Services are not immune to trends in society. Cultural pressures over the last two decades have, for example, resulted in the military changing their policy on deploying women in combat roles and employing homosexuals.[3] Training regimes have had to be modified to take account of deteriorating fitness levels among youngsters; greater effort is being made to recruit people from the ethnic minorities; and recruiters have had to react to the growing number of young people who wish to complete degrees before making career decisions.

The Royal Navy is experiencing difficulty both in recruiting and retaining officers in some branches. Notably, there is a marked shortage of potential engineer officers in the marketplace and the retention of executive officers is particularly problematical. The reasons for these deficiencies are complex and various but the situation might be alleviated if more flexible employment practices were adopted.

At the same time, the cry for public bodies to adopt commercial best practice is widespread. Cross-pollination of skills and experience between the public and private sectors is desirable, if not readily achievable. Increased mobility between the Services, other public organisations and commercial bodies would be one way of spreading and sharing corporate knowledge and might also conform with societal trends towards a more mobile and flexible workforce. This chapter will review the impact on the Royal Navy officer corps of the trend in civilian working practices away from a long term career within one organisation and towards an emphasis on self-development and employment mobility. It will focus on the executive, engineering and supply and secretariat branches and will identify some threats and opportunities that arise from the civilian trend towards portfolio careers.

TRENDS IN WORKING PRACTICES

Much has been written over the past decade about the 'end of the career'[4] and commentators have asserted that holding down a job inside a large organisation is fast becoming the privilege of a minority. Handy, for example, argues that:

> "Work no longer means, for everyone, having a 'job' with an employer. As organisations disperse and contract, more and more of us will be working for ourselves, often by ourselves."[5]

He believes that, as firms continue to contract and concentrate on core activities, the opportunities for career progression within a single organisation decline.[6]

It has been suggested that there are four different career concepts[7] that meet the particular requirements of both employees and employers:

- The *linear* **career** is, perhaps the more traditional career. It involves progressive steps up a hierarchical organisation to positions of increasing authority and responsibility. Employees are motivated by power and achievement. This model is deeply rooted in the value that cultures such as those in the US and the West place on upward mobility.

- The *expert* **career** calls for an employee to make a lifelong commitment to one occupational field, with a focus on refining and developing knowledge and skills. Any progression is in the form of apprentice, through journeyman, to master. The nature of experts' work is an integral part of their self-identity. They tend to seek self-

117

actualisation through achieving expertise, and value security and stability as an environment in which to realise it.

- In the *spiral* **career** employees periodically move across occupational areas or disciplines, typically every seven to ten years. This gives them sufficient time to achieve in-depth competence in a field that they can draw on in their next incarnation. A commercial example of a spiral move would be from engineering or research into product development or marketing. The main motivations for these people are personal development and creativity.

- The *transitory* **career** consists of a succession of moves from one area of employment to other very different fields. These moves might take place every three to five years. This transitory career tends to suit people who are looking for variety and independence.

The response of an organisation to changing employment trends need not be a wholesale shift away from structure and stability to free-form, malleable arrangements. In reality a pluralistic approach may be appropriate.[8] Such an approach would recognise that there are measures of career success other than hierarchical position and organisations could benefit by accommodating people whose motivations differ. Brousseau *et al.* summarised the key features of the four career concepts (Figure 1).

FIGURE 1
FOUR CAREER CONCEPTS

Key Features and Motives

	Linear	Expert	Spiral	Transitory
Direction of movement	Upward	Little movement	Lateral	Lateral
Duration of stay	Variable	Life	7–10 years	3–5 years
Key motives	Power, achievement	Expertise, security	Personal growth, creativity	Variety, independence

Source: Brousseau, Driver, Eneroth and Larsson[9]

PORTFOLIO FEATURES OF THE CURRENT ROYAL NAVY OFFICER'S CAREER

In the Royal Navy each branch has a structure of appointments that provides career development for individuals while maintaining the operational effectiveness of the Service. The structure is designed such that officers change posts every two years or so, thereby learning new skills and applying them practically. This section will outline the typical portfolio of experience that an officer can hope to acquire, and the opportunities that exist for cross-pollination of expertise with other organisations.

The first two years of a typical officer's career will be taken up with training ashore and at sea. This will involve general naval training common to all branches, and branch-specific professional training to prepare the officer for his or her first two-year appointment, usually to a ship or squadron. The skills learned during this phase, both technical and managerial, enable the individual to carry out roles such as a bridge watchkeeper, deputy engineer or assistant secretary. There is a number of common appointments that can be carried out by officers of any branch, such as military assistants to senior officers, recruiting jobs and diplomatic duties, but the mainstream career paths of executive, engineer and supply and secretariat officers tend to diverge.

Executive

The typical executive officer's career path,[10] predominantly based at sea, comprises a series of eighteen to twenty-four month appointments. Progression to the command of a frigate or destroyer involves developing the ability to manoeuvre, fight and manage a ship, and lead her crew. Appointments to various ships could involve watchkeeping, a spell as a navigator, an appointment in the training organisation and jobs as a warfare officer. Qualifications such as pilot and ships' diver are obviously transferable and much of the managerial expertise acquired would be pertinent outside of the military environment. Some of the technical skills have parallels with those employed in, for example, the Merchant Navy, and work is in train to furnish executive officers with appropriate certification where practical.[11]

However, many of the technical competencies are difficult to apply to the civilian world.[12] Lieutenant Commanders with the potential for promotion can expect to spend a year on the Advanced Combined Staff Course (ACSC), during which time they can read for an MA in Defence Studies. Following a command appointment, perhaps in an officer's late thirties or early forties, an individual could expect to move into management posts within the Service and MOD that would require many of the same administrative, HRM and organisational skills as civilian managers.

Engineer

An engineer officer's development is less predictable.[13] Like the executive officer, general organisational and managerial skills will be grown during a succession of two-year appointments leading to charge as a Lieutenant Commander. Unlike the executive officer, there is more scope for engineers to gain a broad experience of other disciplines. An officer may also read for an MSc, attend the ACSC or read for an MDA; some even manage to take two masters degrees. Following a charge appointment, by which time chartered status could have been achieved, an individual would hope to be promoted. The engineer is then expected to become more specialised and concentrate on two or three areas of expertise, such as corporate management or policy development.

The portfolio of skills would therefore continue to grow but become more focused. A number of appointments, such as those in acquisition, require more continuity than others and so lead to a longer tenure.[14] Some officers are suspicious that extended appointments in Integrated Project Teams (IPTs) may damage promotion prospects, and it is too early to say whether the development of deeper expertise and skills that are closely aligned with the civilian world will be seen as a compensation for a narrower portfolio.[15]

Supply and Secretariat

The career development of the supply and secretariat officer is, if anything, less predictable than that for the engineer.[16] A cycle of two-yearly appointments remains the basis of the structure, but the officer can potentially build a very wide portfolio of experience and skills. Apart from the mainstream specialisations of law, management accountancy and information systems, supply and secretariat officers can be given appointments that include logistics, MOD support, training, and secretary or supply officer to an establishment or ship. Officers with potential for promotion would attend the ACSC and there are opportunities for other postgraduate training such as an MDA or MBA. Breadth of experience is seen as extremely important and the use of career templates is shunned because of their prescriptive and potentially restrictive nature.

CROSS–POLLINATION OF EXPERTISE

There is recognition within the Royal Navy that there is value to be gained through contacts with the other Services, other nations' armed forces, the Civil Service and commercial organisations.[17] Michael Bett believed that:

> "... the Armed Forces and their personnel would benefit from more exchanges and secondments with the civilian sector. Such schemes would engender a greater awareness and understanding of business and management practice, and would broaden the experience of those involved. These schemes should also give the commercial world better awareness of the Armed Forces and the quality of their personnel, and would result in a cross-pollination of ideas."[18]

For the purposes of this discussion, cross-pollination of expertise will be broken down into exchanges, secondments, unpaid leave, career breaks and mid-career entry.

Exchanges

The principle of exchanges between the Royal Navy, the other two services and the armed forces of allied nations is firmly established. Such arrangements encourage links, foster understanding and facilitate the interchange of ideas. Reciprocal agreements involving personnel of similar status and skills enable relatively simple bureaucratic processes to be used to administer arrangements such as travelling expenses, subsistence, allowances, liability for injury, salary and pension.[19]

Exchanges with commercial organisations are more problematical and the author's research uncovered no recent examples of their use. Administrative issues such as those described above, though not intractable, would be dealt with on a case-by-case basis as no reliable formulae exist within the MOD.[20] Particularly troublesome is the question of liability for injury in the event that civilians are employed in a front-line environment such as a ship. Moreover, given the amount of specialist training that officers require before they are appointed to the front-line, there are doubts regarding the time it would take a civilian to become effective in those surroundings.[21]

There may be scope for using the Royal Naval Reserve (RNR) as a mechanism for employing civilians under military regulations, and civilians destined for an exchange could gain an understanding of the Service through receiving staff training.[22] However, such measures would require significant investment on the part of the civilian organisation and a compelling commercial case would have to be made for them to be justified.

Nevertheless, there are some precedents for the employment of civilians within the military. There are Royal Fleet Auxiliary (RFA) officers serving on the staff of Flag Officers and civilian contractors have in the past been deployed to war zones to solve equipment problems.[23] Also, as the Smart Procurement Initiative (SPI) gathers pace and Integrated Project Teams (IPTs) develop, there is an increasingly strong case for defence contractors to improve their comprehension of military customers as much as for the Services to better understand industry.[24] Industry has shown interest in attachments to the MOD, and BAe Systems has been particularly keen to provide personnel to sit on working groups.[25]

Secondments

There are numerous posts within the MOD that can be occupied both by military personnel and Civil Servants. There are also many appointments within the MOD and its agencies that explicitly call for military experience. Often, these MOD appointments involve close contact with industry, for example in the Defence Procurement Agency (DPA) and Defence Logistics Organisation (DLO). Such appointments, which provide valuable exposure to non-military processes and practices, are of benefit to an individual officer's portfolio of skills and contribute to the Royal Navy's corporate knowledge. Direct secondments to commercial organisations, however, are scarce.[26]

Secondments do not have the same natural element of reciprocity as exchanges and so some other quid pro quo is needed. Generally, there is a trade-off between the costs and benefits of the arrangement to both of the organisations involved. Although secondments of Royal Navy officers are not common, instances can be found where either: the Service has borne the costs; the organisation receiving an officer has absorbed all expenses; or liability has been shared.

Examples of secondments where costs have been borne by the Royal Navy involve Shell UK and Cadbury-Schweppes. In the former, which is still active, an executive Commander is seconded for six weeks to Shell's headquarters to study an area of mutual interest. A similar scheme with P&O is currently under consideration.[27] The Cadbury-Schweppes arrangement, which has lapsed, involved the five-month secondment of a Lieutenant Commander to the European supply and travel division.

It is unlikely that an officer will be made available for a long secondment unless his or her services are paid for. Such a case arose when a Commander engineer sought permission to apply for a publicly advertised post on the board of the Defence Aircraft Repair Agency (DARA).[28] Permission was granted, the Grade 6 post was secured, the individual was granted the acting higher rank of Captain and the DARA reimbursed the Service for the full capitation cost of a Captain.[29] DARA benefited by employing the best person for the job and, it is hoped, the Royal Navy will benefit from the officer's experience when he returns to the Service.[30]

An area in which the use of secondments is likely to become more widespread is acquisition management. As the Acquisition Stream (AS) develops and the appointment of IPT leaders is exclusively by selection, commercial experience will become vital. Colonel Chris Coates, the Team Leader for operations in the Acquisition Management Cell, observed that:

> "There is no doubt that if military officers want to play at the highest level, other than the posts that clearly can only ever be military, those who are up for competition are going to have to have this broader [commercial] experience."[31]

The only AS secondments operating at the moment involve Civil Service personnel. The view prevalent within MOD-industry human resources working groups is that a start should be made by upping the number of attachments (that is, in Civil Service parlance, periods of three months or less),[32] if attachments are seen as successful, secondments should grow out of them.

Unpaid leave

Other than the statutory requirements for maternity and paternity leave, there is a facility for unpaid leave in the Royal Navy. Granted in exceptional circumstances where paid leave is not deemed appropriate,[33] it is used rarely by ratings and hardly ever by officers.[34] Examples of its use would be:

- Business or estate difficulties if no other appropriate person is available to deal with them

- Activities considered beneficial to the Service, such as an unofficial expedition

- Any other activity that would not warrant release from the Service, such as leave to join a husband or wife for a foreign appointment.

During unpaid leave an individual receives no pay, benefits or allowances from the Crown and accrues no seniority for the purposes of promotion, pay or pension.[35]

Career breaks

There are no formal arrangements within the Royal Navy for taking career breaks. Officers who leave the Service can apply to rejoin with the same seniority they had at retirement and, if there are vacancies, they have not been away for too long and their record is good, they may be accepted.[36] However, unless the organisation is growing – and that has been uncommon in the Royal Navy over the last fifty years – the need to bring people back at senior levels is rare and will occur only where there are particular skill shortages.[37] The greatest officer shortages currently are among Lieutenants, and indications are that they tend to leave for reasons that the Service would find difficult to change. Recent data from Premature Voluntary Release (PVR) surveys[38] found that the most important reason for resigning given by Lieutenants was the desire to live at home. The next three most important reasons were:

- The kind of Service jobs they could expect in the future

- The amount of separation from family and friends

- The wish to start another career.

A questionnaire is sent out to officers who have resigned their commission, one-year after they leave the Service, to monitor how they have settled into civilian life.[39] No subsequent monitoring is carried out though, so no hard data exists that would confirm or refute the belief that Lieutenants in shortage categories would not wish to resume a naval career.

Mid-career entry

Mid-career entry, that is joining the Service at a level of seniority greater than that which would be awarded to new entrants, is possible when an applicant has relevant previous military experience. There have, for example, been instances of officers transferring to the Royal Navy from Commonwealth navies and retaining their seniority. Other than that though, apart from specialists such as medical doctors, dentists and clerics, civilians recruited into the Service are not given credit for their previous experience. A twenty-six-year-old currently joins the Royal Navy with the same seniority as a twenty-one-year-old,[40] with no account taken of his or her former employment and the benefits to the organisation that their knowledge and ideas may bring.

A MODEL FOR THE ROYAL NAVY

Recently the Royal Navy has embarked upon a high level examination of its current manning levels. It appears to have similar aims to this chapter in that it '...is looking for innovative ideas'.[41] This Strategic Manpower Review (SMR) aims '...to deliver a manning process to meet operational capability in the short, medium and long term which is both achievable and affordable'.[42] The discussion so far would seem to indicate that the Royal Navy's manning process would benefit from being more flexible in some of its employment policies. Career mobility has become increasingly prevalent over the last two decades and today's employees are acutely aware of a responsibility to manage their own professional lives.

Brousseau, Driver, Eneroth and Larsson's 1994 analysis[43] of career concepts, outlined above, can be used as a basis for assessing the suitability of the current officers' career structure for accommodating trends in employment mobility. Where the present structure is found lacking, appropriate changes can be identified.

STRATEGIC AIM

This analysis will take as a starting point the proposal that career structures, based on a blend of career concepts, can be derived to suit the strategic aim of a business. Though the strategic directions and advantages put forward in Figure 2 are clearly designed with commercial businesses in mind, with a little interpretation they can be applied to the Royal Navy, possibly as part of its current review

Growth

It would be difficult to argue that the business of the Royal Navy is growing. Over the last fifteen years its uniformed manpower has shrunk by thirty-eight per cent[45] and real defence expenditure has fallen by thirty per cent.[46] There may be areas of growth within the Service, driven perhaps by adopting new technologies such as IT, or organisational change such as the formation of the DPA and DLO, but the overall trend has been shrinkage. The Service's strategic advantage in the international arena does not come from economies of scale. Consequently, a predominantly *linear* career culture would not appear to be the most apt to meet the Royal Navy's strategic direction.

FIGURE 2
LINKING ORGANISATIONAL STRATEGIES TO CAREER CULTURES

Strategic Direction	Strategic Advantage	Organisational Career Culture
Growth	Low Price High volume/low cost	Linear
Maintain position	Quality Reliability	Expert
Diversification	Creativity Innovation	Spiral
Entrepreneurial opportunity New market creation	Speed Novelty Ease of use	Transitory

Source: Brousseau, Driver, Eneroth and Larsson[44]

Diversification

Despite healthy rivalry between the three Armed Services, it is not the Royal Navy's place to diversify into the roles of the Army and the Royal Air Force. Notwithstanding the existence of a seagoing army (the Royal Marines) and air force (the Fleet Air Arm), the Royal Navy's core competence remains the projection of maritime power.[47] However, though peripheral to the Service's main business, increasing budgetary awareness has resulted in the creation of a number of schemes that use spare military capacity to generate income. Arrangements such as the 'Flagship'[48] training initiative could be viewed as a degree of diversification. Creativity and innovation, hallmarks of a *spiral* culture, are needed among the officer corps but they are not its most important strengths.

Entrepreneurial opportunity and new market creation

During peacetime, the author is aware of no compelling need

in the Royal Navy for the entrepreneurial skills of a *transitory* culture. In wartime, however, there may well be a role for the free spirit who tries novel approaches and is willing to take risks.

Maintain position

The Royal Navy's strategy falls most readily into the category of maintaining its position. Having been given its direction by the Strategic Defence Review (SDR),[49] and without any other clear idea of what the future holds,[50] the Service can do little other than implement those changes outlined in the SDR and consolidate its reputation for reliability and quality. The Royal Navy's strategic aim seems to best suit the *expert* career culture.

THE ROYAL NAVY'S CURRENT ORGANISATIONAL CULTURE

The pluralistic structure described above is not too far removed from that in place within the Royal Navy today. There has been some flattening of the hierarchical pyramid, though not to the extent that was recommended by Michael Bett,[51] and all officers joining on the Three Tier Commission have similar opportunities for promotion to the highest ranks.[52] Work is in hand to implement a form of performance-related pay[53] and there are some opportunities for broadening appointments for officers. The evolution of the DPA and DLO is providing scope for some officers to work in the inter-disciplinary environment of IPTs, and the Service has stated its commitment to learning.[54] Finally, the Special Forces and other deeply expert teams could be seen as providing limited opportunities for more independent souls.

The need for change

If employment concepts are considered to lie on the continuum shown at Figure 3, the employment trends that have been described point to a shift within the general population to the right.

FIGURE 3
CONTINUUM OF EMPLOYMENT CONCEPTS

Linear	*Expert*	*Spiral*	*Transitory*

Employment population trend

However, an analysis of the Royal Navy's organisational requirements indicates a need for predominantly *expert* and *linear* types. The Service would seem to have a choice between reinforcing its appeal to *linear* and *expert* employees, in order to better compete for a shrinking pool, or to adapt its culture to take advantage of the relatively high availability of individuals tending to the *spiral* and *transitory* concepts. The ideal organisational culture would, of course, incorporate a mixture of opportunities that made the most effective use of all the available manpower assets.

AN ACCOMMODATION OF DIFFERENT CAREER CONCEPTS

The accommodation of each of the career concepts needs to be considered separately:

The *linear* officer

Despite some flattening of the organisation, there would still appear to be an adequately tall and well-defined hierarchy to satisfy the ambitions of *linear* officers for power and achievement. The introduction of performance-related pay, if well structured, should further appeal to this group. Whether opportunities for promotion come early enough to retain these officers in sufficient numbers is a debate outside of the scope of this piece. The *linear* tenure is characterised as indeterminate and their reasons for leaving would govern whether they could be tempted back. For example, someone who leaves because the system cannot meet his or her ambitions for advancement or salary is unlikely to return. Conversely, an officer who elects to take a three to five year break to raise a family may be inclined to rejoin, provided that his or her ambitions for promotion and power can be accommodated.

The *expert* officer

The re-negotiation of the Service's psychological contract with its officers, whereby a 'job for life' became a thing of the past, will have damaged the appeal of the Royal Navy to those *expert* career officers drawn to security and stability. Nonetheless, the Service still offers a career that is secure relative to the majority of the rest of the employment market, so these officers would appear to be reasonably well accommodated. However, reward for achievement is still firmly linked to promotion and this does not ideally suit the *expert*. The de-linking of pay from rank should go some way towards remedying the situation but details have yet to emerge of exactly how the new system will be implemented.[55] Any erosion of the Service's fringe benefits is likely to affect the motivation of this group of officers in particular.

Expert officers, if offered security, recognition and the opportunity to develop their expertise, are unlikely to wish to leave the Service. Those who do resign may be tempted back if whatever caused their dissatisfaction is subsequently remedied.

The *spiral* officer

It is in the attraction and retention of the Royal Navy officer who matches the *spiral* career concept that organisational changes are most needed. The teamwork, personnel development and creativity that this group could offer, together with their relative dominance of the current employment market, should ensure their cultivation as a valuable segment of the officer corps. These officers would already be attracted to the variety of jobs available in the Service, particularly in the engineering and supply and secretariat branches, and would thrive if the opportunities for lateral assignments and creative latitude were expanded. Their medium-term career outlook could be accommodated were they to be targeted as initial recruits straight from university or, subsequently, in their late twenties following seven years or so in pursuit of another career. In the latter case, a naval career would have to be seen as a natural developmental step and they would expect to be given credit for what they had already achieved.

Spiral officers who were recruited early could be expected to want to move to pastures new after seven to ten years. It may be possible to accommodate such a move within the Service by offering traditional opportunities for personal growth, such as postgraduate training and a progression from engineering to acquisition management. However, those officers who choose to leave the Service to seek development elsewhere may well be willing to return to the fold after seven years or so if they leave on a positive note and, again, are given credit for achievement on their return.

The *transitory* officer

The *transitory* officer is the wild card of the pack. His or her strengths of adaptability and innovation could be vital in time of war and would be valuable in peacetime. However, for the return on training investment to be cost-effective, a three to five year period of service is insufficient.[56] Unless these officers' need for independence and short-term rewards can be met through specialist appointments, excitement and the variety of Service life, it is difficult to see how else they can be accommodated in any numbers.

SUGGESTED REFINEMENTS AND CHANGES

The analysis suggests a number of refinements of, and changes to, the Royal Navy's organisational culture:

- **Promotion and pay**
  The award of promotion and performance-related pay must be thoughtfully implemented such that *linear* officers' need for advancement and the trappings of rank are balanced with the *expert's* desire for recognition and fringe benefits. Care must be taken that the two groups are not seen to belong to different strata, with the non-*linear* stream seen as second-class.[57] Such a balancing act is, of course, more easily described than achieved.

- **Fringe benefits**
  The consequence of any erosion of fringe benefits should be given particular consideration in the light of the marked motivational effect they would be likely to have on the core, *expert* officer.

- **Mature recruits**

  Consideration should be given to the attraction of *spiral* officers, seven to ten years after they embark on their first career, by targeting recruits at, say, age twenty-seven to thirty and awarding them seniority concordant with their experience. A career in the Royal Navy may thereby become more attractive to this group and their experience would contribute to the Service's corporate knowledge. Provided that the seniority awarded were at the Lieutenant level, subsequent promotion would be by selection and, based on merit, should not disadvantage the cohort of serving officers.

- **Career broadening**

  Consideration should be given to expanding broadening opportunities such as secondments to civilian organisations. This measure would increase the appeal of a Service career both to *spiral* and *expert* officers, and so aid recruitment and retention. Cross-pollination of experience would contribute to corporate knowledge, and public awareness of the Royal Navy would be improved. Moreover, success in areas such as the DPA and DLO might depend on the sort of commercial insight that could best be gained through close contact with industry. Return of service or other hooks could be used to ensure an adequate return on investment but, it is hoped, when combined with the other recommended refinements and changes, continuing a Service career would become generally more attractive.

  Civilian appointments would not appeal to all officers, particularly those with *linear* motivations, because it is possible that time spent out of the mainstream might slow promotion. However, individuals should be given the opportunity to choose their own career path having made an assessment of its likely impact on what they personally wish to achieve, both at work and in their private lives.

- **Career breaks**

  The facility to take career breaks would suit officers belonging to all career cultures. The continuing trend of women returning to the workplace after child-rearing has been followed by a growing number of fathers who want to play a more active role in raising their offspring. It must be in the Service's interest to capitalise on the opportunity to re-employ trained officers who wish to resume their naval careers.

Moreover, some *spiral* officers might be attracted to rejoin provided that they were given credit for their experience and were offered a worthwhile career path. The numbers involved may not be large, but efforts by the Service to accommodate them would pay dividends in terms of recouping some return on investment.

Moreover, in the view of the author, officers that were able to leave without necessarily 'burning their boats' would feel less inclined to convince themselves that the job was not for them. They would consequently carry a more positive and sympathetic image of the Royal Navy into civilian life, and the Service's standing as an employer would rise.[58]

Long career breaks of, say, two to five years could carry no guarantee of re-employment but the Service would undertake to take the officer back if a vacancy existed. For shorter breaks, unpaid leave could be more widely used. Officers taking breaks should be kept abreast of developments in the Service through the provision of regular briefing packs. As in the case for career broadening, individuals would have to make their own assessment of the effects that breaks would have on their careers and lives, but they should have that choice. The mechanisms for career breaks are largely already in place. There is an opportunity to repackage them in order to improve the perception of the Royal Navy as a flexible employer.

- **Military ethos**
  In a recent article, Commodore Massey illustrated the dichotomy between maintaining military ethos and accommodating cultural trends.[59] Just because a trend exists in the civilian world does not mean that it should be reflected in the military. In fact, to do so could be harmful. As General Sir Michael Rose put it:

  "...soldiers are not merely civilians in uniform: they form a distinctive group within our society that needs a different set of moral values in order to succeed in circumstances which differ greatly from those in civilian life...Today, our military ethos...is being actively destroyed by a mixture of social change within our own society and new national and international legislation."[60]

Nonetheless, there can be little argument that there needs to be some correlation between the sub-culture of the Armed Forces and the wider society that they represent and from which their numbers are drawn. A former Minister for the Armed Forces stated that:

"Armed Forces that better represent the society that they exist to defend will be better able to meet the challenges of the 21st century."[61]

Reductions in defence spending, recruiting difficulties, criticism of military policies and a low level of public familiarity are all signs that the national consensus for defence has subtly eroded.[62] The Services' engagement with society has reduced as their visibility has faded. As the Rt. Hon. Dr John Reid observed:

"In the foreseeable future we will live in a society composed and governed by those whose lives have been largely untouched in any direct personal fashion by military experience."[63]

The author contends that the refinements and changes he has proposed would do nothing to harm military ethos in fact they would:

• Improve officers' conditions of service

• Have a positive effect on recruitment and retention

• Help the Royal Navy to re-engage with the public it serves.

CONCLUSIONS

There are benefits to be gained by the Royal Navy in adopting more flexible employment practices in the areas of secondments, exchanges, career breaks, unpaid leave and mid-career entry. Direct benefits to the Service might include:

- An expansion and better dispersal of corporate knowledge

- Exposure to best commercial practice

- Access to larger pool of potential recruits

- The development of a happier, better-motivated work-force.

Indirect benefits could be:

- An improvement in the Service's reputation as an employer

- A public relations and recruiting boost that would come from a wider and more positive exposure of the general public to Royal Navy personnel

- The ability to better-accommodate changing environ-mental forces.

Even though relatively few officers might wish take advantage of the opportunities offered by a more liberal regime, their contribution to corporate knowledge should prove most valuable. Moreover, a general awareness that such opportunities existed should have a positive effect on morale in general and the Service's image in particular.

A career in the Royal Navy offers security that is rare in the commercial world. If that commitment on the part of the Service were tempered by a demonstrable will not to unnecessarily restrict its employees' mobility, a potent recruitment and retention tool would be forged. The career structure of the officer corps is fundamentally sound, broadly in step with progressive management thinkers and there are no significant legal or procedural obstacles to increasing the flexibility of employment. There is a need, however, for some refinement of the organisational culture but the changes that are needed are within the Service's own control.

The Smart Procurement Initiative (SPI) is a key driver of the need for officers to gain experience of commercial practices and processes. However, high calibre officers will not be attracted to the Acquisition Stream (AS) unless the Service's career culture is developed to meet their ambitions and needs.

Therefore there is a need for a cultural change within the officer corps to accommodate not only civilian employment trends, but also its own evolution from a tall hierarchical pyramid to a flatter organisation offering fewer promotion opportunities. The Service will find it increasingly difficult to recruit and retain high calibre officers if it does not cultivate an environment that is equally comfortable for those seeking promotion and those motivated by lateral development. Such a cultural change needs careful manipulation of promotion, non-financial rewards, job security and recognition of the value of civilian experience. The proportional mix of these ingredients will determine the type of officer that is recruited and retained.

NOTES

1. Handy, C., *The Empty Raincoat* (Arrow Books, London, 1994) p.71.
2. Caulkin, Simon, 'The New Avengers', *Management Today* (London, November 1995) p.44.
3. Ministry of Defence, *New Code of Conduct for Armed Services Personnel* (London, HMSO, 12 January 2000) pp.1–6.
4. Anon, 'The Future of Work', *The Economist* (London, 29 January 2000) p.113.
5. Handy, C., op. cit. p.74.
6. Ibid., p.114.
7. Brousseau, K. R. and Driver, M. J., 'Enhancing informed choice: A career-concepts approach to career advisement', *Selections* 10/3 (Spring 1994) pp.24–34.
8. Brousseau, K. R., Driver, M. J., Eneroth, K. and Larsson, R., 'Career pandemonium: Realigning organizations and individuals', *The Academy of Management Executive* (Ada, November 1996) p.57.
9. Ibid., p.58.
10. Based on Naval Manning Agency career templates provided to the author on 5 July 2000 by Cdr M. Mansergh.
11. Mansergh, Cdr M., DNOA(X)/ CDRX, telephone interview with the author 5 July 2000.
12. Bone, Cdr D., executive officer seconded to Shell UK, telephone interview with the author 15 May 2000.
13. Based on Naval Manning Agency career templates provided to the author on 2 June 2000 by Lt Cdr C. Harvey, DNOA(E)/ESM.
14. Coates, Col. C., Team Leader – Operations, Acquisition Management Cell, interview with the author, 15 May 2000.
15. Ibid.
16. Based on guidance given to the author on 27 June 2000 during a telephone interview with Cdr J. Litchfield, DNMS (Supply Branch Manager), Naval Manning Agency.
17. Williams, Cdre S., Chief Naval Officer Appointing, interview with the author, 4 May 2000.
18. Bett, Michael, CBE, *Independent Review of the Armed Forces' Manpower, Career and Remuneration Structures* (HMSO, 1995) p.42.
19. Graham, K., NMA Sec2, interview with the author, 17 May 2000.
20. Ibid.

21. Williams, Cdre S., op. cit.
22. Ibid.
23. Ibid.
24. Coates, Col. C., op. cit.
25. Ibid.
26. Williams, Cdre S., op. cit.
27. Redford, Cdr K., Staff Officer Common Appointments, NMA, interview with the author, 9 May 2000.
28. Williams, Cdre S., op. cit.
29. Graham, K., op. cit.
30. Williams, Cdre S., op. cit.
31. Coates, Col. C., op. cit.
32. Ibid.
33. BR 8587, *Naval Leave and Travel Regulations* (change 12, 1996) Article 0507.
34. Davies, Cdr B., SOA(Coord), CNOA, telephone interview with the author, 10 July 2000.
35. BR 8587, op. cit.
36. Ministry of Defence, *Royal Navy: Entry into the Engineering Branch*, Career Guidance 4 (Naval Manning Agency, August 1998) p.12.
37. Williams, Cdre S., op. cit.
38. RN Officer PVR Interim Data – June 1st 1999 to February 1st 2000, provided by Cdr B. Davies, DNOA/SOA(Coord), during an interview with the author, 8 May 2000.
39. Davies, Cdr B., SOA(Coord), CNOA, telephone interview with the author, 8 May 2000.
40. Ministry of Defence, *Royal Navy: Entry into the Engineering Branch* op. cit.
41. Williams, Cdr S., Chief Naval Officer Appointing, interview with author 4 May 2000.
42. The aim was stated at the inaugural SMR workshop held at Victory Building, Portsmouth, 8 May 2000.
43. Brousseau, Driver, Eneroth, and Larsson, 'Career pandemonium', op. cit., p.57.
44. Ibid., p.61.
45. MOD, *UK Defence Statistics, 1999* (London, The Stationery Office, 1999) Table 2.8.
46. Ibid., Table 1.3.
47. BR 1806, *The Fundamentals of British Maritime Doctrine* (London: HMSO, 1995) p.49.
48. In 1996 Flagship Training signed a fifteen year agreement with the MOD to enter into a partnering arrangement with the Royal Navy's recruiting and training agency (NRTA) to provide training to foreign navies and the civil market, http://www.flagshiptraining. co.uk/about.htm.
49. *Strategic Defence Review*, Cm.3999 (HMSO, July 1998) http://www.army. mod.uk/army/press/events/sdr.ht.
50. Williams, Cdre S., op. cit.
51. Bett, Michael, CBE, *Independent Review of the Armed Forces' Manpower, Career and Remuneration Structures* (HMSO, 1995) pp.16–23.
52. 2SL/CNH, 'The New Officer Structure for the Naval Service', *Three Tier Commission Information Booklet* (Command HQ Graphics, 1998).
53. Bett, Michael, CBE, op. cit., p.47.
54. DNSC, 'Lifelong Learning', *DNSC Brief 2000 – Education and Resettlement* (DNSC, June 2000) http://132.0.15.90/resource/2sl/directorates/dnsc_dnpfs/dnsc_brief/education.htm.
55. Bett, Michael, CBE, op. cit., pp.3–5 and 3–6.
56. Williams, Cdre S., op. cit.

57. Brousseau, Driver, Eneroth and Larsson, op. cit., p.60.
58. Tamkin, P., Psychologist, Institute of Employment Studies, interview with the author, 19 May 2000.
59. Massey, Cdre A. M., 'Ethos, Consensus and UK Defence in the 21st Century', *The Naval Review*, 88/1 (January 2000) p.3.
60. Rose, General Sir Michael, 'How Soon Could Our Army Lose a War?', *Daily Telegraph* (16 December 1997).
61. Reid, The Hon. Dr J., Minister of the Armed Forces, House of Commons Adjournment debate on racism in the Armed Forces, Hansard (22 January 1998) column 1246.
62. Massey, Commodore A. M., op. cit., p.5.
63. Reid, The Hon. Dr J., 'The Armed Forces and Society', *RUSI Journal*, 142/2 (London, April 1997) p.31, cited in: Massey, Cdre A. M., op. cit., p.3.

10

Independent Representation –
The Time is Right

RICHARD BARTLE
Cranfield University, Royal Military College of Science

INTRODUCTION

It is now more than five years since the publication of the Bett
Report on the Armed Forces' Manpower, Career and
Remuneration Structures[1] in which Sir Michael called for
servicemen to argue the case for 'an organisation to represent
their collective concerns'.[2] He suggested that the issue should
be 'freely debated within the Services' but since then very
little has happened. The debate has not occurred. Yet the
evidence of Bett's report and various pieces of research both
published and unpublished is that there is substantial
support for independent representation throughout a large
proportion of the Armed Forces.[3] So, the question must be
asked – why has there been no debate?

One of the difficulties for Servicemen and women is that
they are prevented by Queen's Regulations[4] from becoming
involved in discussions on issues which are sensitive,
politically or otherwise. Eric Joyce has been one of the few
serving officers to challenge this rule and to argue the case for
independent representation.[5] His subsequent fall from grace
is unlikely to encourage many others to voice their opinions
in public.[6] Thus, within the services, the debate called for by
Bett is only feasible to those service personnel who, like
Joyce, are prepared to run the risk of a blighted career.

Perhaps the only recourse would be for some brave souls
to resort to the law (as did homosexual and lesbian
personnel)[7] in order to change the system. The homosexuals
and lesbians, though, had a great deal of support from
outside the military and also organised their own
representative body – Rank Outsiders. Those contemplating
similar action to achieve independent representation outside

the chain of command, however, are likely to be caught in a 'Catch 22' situation in that they would be arguing for independent representation but would probably need the support of an independent representative body to mount a successful challenge.

During the late 1970s some unions did express an interest in recruiting servicemen and women[8] and today, arguably, some might still be interested in recruiting them. But Armed Forces personnel do not seem to want a trade union. Indeed, research results indicate that while there is substantial support for independent representation there is just as much opposition to that representation being by a trade union.[9] The format that seems to have the most backing is for a body similar to the Police Federation that would not have the right to strike but would have the authority to speak on behalf of all ranks.

In some circles it was thought that a breakthrough had occurred in 1979 when Dr John Reid (erstwhile Minister of State for the Armed Forces) said that 'wherever practical and sensible, military law and liberties should reflect the values of contemporary society'.[10] However, this was a remark made when New Labour was in opposition. Since coming to power, the Armed Forces have been exempted from various pieces of employment legislation emanating from Europe.[11] Most importantly, this includes Article 11 of the European Convention for the Protection of Human Rights[12] which says: 'Everyone has the right to freedom of peaceful assembly and to freedom of association with others, including the right to form and to join trade unions for the protection of his interests.' Admittedly, there is an additional proviso that 'this article shall not prevent the imposition of lawful restrictions on the exercise of these rights by members of the Armed Forces, of the police or of the administration of the State'.[13] Nevertheless, many European countries treat members of their Armed Forces as 'citizens in uniform'[14] granting them the same rights as civilians including the right to form and join trade unions.

In this country little has been forthcoming from the government on this matter. However, there have been some significant statements from senior serving and retired officers that, perhaps, give a flavour of present attitudes, General Sir Michael Rose for example, argues that:

"These laws [Article 11, European Convention on Human Rights] are designed to improve civilian employment practices and are entirely inappropriate for soldiers on the battlefield."[15]

While General Sir Roger Wheeler opines that:

"the efficient running of an organisation such as the Army occasionally requires the subjugation of individual rights for the greater good."[16]

If these statements are a true reflection of government policy, there would seem to be little opportunity to introduce independent representation in the Armed Services in UK at present.

But, near silence from the ranks does not mean that either the mood or the motive does not exist. Indeed, the most recent research into attitudes among significant numbers of both officers and other ranks[17] indicates that independent representation is still a 'hot' issue and that the need for servicemen to argue the case for 'an organisation to represent their collective concerns' is as great today as it was in 1995. As the rank and file are unable (for whatever reason) to argue their case it is important that someone makes it for them. Therefore, this chapter will, unashamedly, put the case FOR independent representation in the British Armed Forces. To that end it will examine the roles and functions of both the Police Federation and modern trade unions in the context of life in the military today. Within this framework it will identify the need for independent representation in the Armed Forces and make suggestions as to how that need might be met.

TRADE UNIONS TODAY

Beatrice and Sidney Webb defined a trade union as 'a continuous association of wage earners for the purpose of maintaining or improving the conditions of their working lives'.[18] According to the TUC, 'trade unions developed because working people could not rely on employers to look after their welfare, working conditions and wages unprompted'.[19] To some extent this gives a clearer picture of the functions of trade unions than the traditional right wing assumption that they are merely vehicles for political agitation through industrial action. Indeed, modern trade unions perform a wide array of functions related to most aspects of working life ranging from medical matters to legal representation. Table 1 (opposite) gives a selection of the various functions with examples of the kinds of services provided by modern trade unions.

The table is only intended to give a sample of the services provided and is by no means fully representative of all that trade unions can do for their members today. Nevertheless, the list is impressive and paints a much wider picture than that of the stereotypical concept of the industrial troublemaker epitomised by images of the miners' strike. Indeed, perhaps the most fascinating aspect of modern trade unions is the ways in which they are now working with employers to develop partnerships to improve industrial relations and to work towards the success of the organisation. To that end the TUC Partnership Institute has been set up to encourage employers and trade unions to create long standing relationships that 'focus on the future of the business and improving the working life of employees'.[20] An underlying principle of this initiative is the growth of trust between employers and their workforces in order to create successful partnerships committed to the success of the enterprise.

It is doubtful that military respondents in the various studies were aware of the wide scope of modern trade union functions when they rejected membership of a trade union for the Armed Forces. Many were strongly against any form of strike action[21] which is probably why, having recognised the need for independent representation, they opted for a similar organisation to the Police Federation which has no right to strike.

THE POLICE FEDERATION

The Police Federation of England and Wales is the statutory body that exists to represent the interests of all police officers up to the rank of Chief Inspector. It is not a trade union. Police officers, like military personnel, are not allowed to belong to a trade union or to strike. However, it does exist to negotiate the pay and conditions of service of all members. Ironically, the origins of the Federation can be traced back to the efforts of General Sir Nevil Macready, Commissioner of the

Metropolitan Police Force, to crush the embryonic union responsible for the police strike in August 1918. Initially, Macready set up representative boards to replace the union but their failure resulted in the Desborough Committee's recommendation of the establishment of a representative of body for police officers.[22] This recommendation was embodied in the Police Bill (1919) which increased police pay, prohibited membership of a trade union and set up a Police Federation. The final act of the police union was to call for strike action to wreck the formation of the Federation. This was unsuccessful and the Federation held its first conference in November 1919.

TABLE 1.
FUNCTIONS OF TRADE UNIONS AND EXAMPLES OF THE SERVICES
THEY PROVIDE

Trade Union Functions	Examples
Representations	Pay Pensions Conditions of work Collective bargaining Industrial Action
Legal	Advice Unfair dismissal Health and safety Civil claims Criminal injuries
Discipline	Appeals Advice Representation Framing rules
Medical	Examinations Fees for claims
Personnel	Welfare Personnel issues Discrimination Redundancy Training Pension advice
Partnership	Industrial relations Commitment to success Joint decision making and problem solving Mutual trust

The fundamental structure of the Federation, of separate boards for Constables, Sergeants and Inspectors that would act together on matters of common interest, has not changed since 1919. It has been suggested that this structure was 'based upon the "divide and rule" concept and was designed by the government of the day to fail'.[23] This, of course, has not been the case but the history of the Federation has been one of struggle to maintain its identity and to represent the interests of all three ranks. Nevertheless, since 1955 the Federation has been allowed to levy a voluntary subscription from members and this has enabled the provision of a service that includes: welfare support to members; assistance to those who fall foul of the discipline code; appearance at medical tribunals; providing counselling to those in financial difficulties; assisting members involved in Employment Tribunals; administering members' service facilities; attending meetings of welfare funds; and making sure that those who are ill or injured complete the insurance claims correctly or simply receive regular visits during the time that they are off duty.[24]

All this in addition to the primary function of representation on pay and conditions of service. The members of the police force, like the military, are still prevented by law from joining a trade union or from taking strike action so it is little wonder that this federation model should hold such an attraction to members of the Armed Forces.[25]

THE CASE FOR A MILITARY FEDERATION

The British Armed Forces is a unique organisation that is particularly reliant upon a set of values that have been described as a total open-ended commitment, subordination of the self to the group and the idea of sacrifice of selfish interest, even a willingness to risk losing one's life.[26] Military law prevents service personnel from striking or negotiating over working conditions. Therefore, in return for this open-ended commitment is the expectation of a paternalistic system in which pay, terms and conditions of service, accommodation and even food and clothing are guaranteed and protected by the senior officers. However, this arrangement is unwritten and subjective, based upon the expectations of both parties and founded upon the mutual trust that each will honour their commitment – in other words, a psychological contract. Glaister[27] argues that any change in the psychological contract on the part of the organisation will lead to a re-evaluation by each employee of his or her position within the organisation. Indeed if the psychological contract is broken by either side a redefinition of roles is likely to occur.

Evidence of the breakdown of this relationship has been well documented.[28] Eric Joyce[29] gave his interpretation of the reasons for changes in the psychological contract in his controversial paper for the Fabian Society. The main thrust of his argument was that budgetary changes resulting from the introduction of the New Management Strategy (NMS) placed senior military officers in a new dilemma. Before NMS they could be expected to represent the views of the rank and file to the MoD and those in charge of the financial purse strings. After NMS senior officers became the budget holders with responsibility for local decisions on such matters as accommodation, working life, food and even job design. Thus in place of standard conditions of service dictated from MoD, a situation now exists in which there can be differences in the quality of life for lower ranks depending upon decisions made by local budget managers. Any trust in senior officers as representatives of the concerns of service personnel seems to have been seriously damaged by these changes.

It could be argued, however, that NMS was only the beginning of a series of changes in the psychological contract that have led to a redefinition of the roles of service personnel. Realisation of the Cold War dividend beginning with 'Options for Change'[30] saw major reductions in the size of the Armed Forces. These cutbacks in manpower resulted in a total of 34,600 redundancies across the three services over a period of five years. Such measures were an enormous shock to the Armed Forces who had never had to face the prospect of redundancy before. The general impression until 'Options for Change' had been that a serviceman's psychological contract assumed unlimited liability, up to and including the readiness to sacrifice himself, and in return he had the guarantee of job security. Thus, as one Colonel admitted, this round of redundancies hit morale and trust very hard.[31]

Subsequently any residual trust and morale has been seriously tried by further changes in the relationship between the expectations of the employees and the offerings of the employer. High on the list of these has been the introduction of modern commercial methods such as the creation of 'Next Steps Agencies'. These are halfway houses between public and private sector that are based upon suitable military organisations but run for a profit. Often run by civilians, these agencies have servicemen and women working alongside civilians and doing the same or comparable work. Arguably, this is far from the expectations of most service personnel who could find similar work in 'civvy street' without joining the Armed Forces.

In addition, the MoD has 'a poor record in the field of employment welfare'.[32] Examples such as the problems over Gulf War Syndrome and compensation for injuries in Bosnia[33] have added fuel to the fire and strengthened the perception that senior officers can no longer be trusted to represent servicemen/women. The conclusion, according to Joyce,[34] is that independent representation outside the chain of command is needed to redress the balance.

Indeed, recent research[35] shows that Armed Forces personnel want to have more say in policies on such matters as pay, allowances, career development, single soldiers' accommodation, married quarters and postings and that they favour some form of independent representation to achieve this. The overwhelming consensus is that this can best be achieved through an organisation similar to the Police Federation. The Federation provides its members with all the functions and services listed in Table 1 with the one exception of industrial action (more especially, it is prohibited by law from taking strike action). Consequently, the case for a military federation might usefully be examined further by considering each of the functions in the light of recent personnel management problems to see what contribution, if any, might be made by a federation to improve relations.

Representation

The present system of representation in the Armed Forces is based upon the chain of command. It relies upon officers passing information upwards and representing the needs of their subordinates. This is only half of the picture, though. Officers are the main channel of organisational communication and as well as communicating their sub-ordinates' requirements upwards, also have the responsibility of communicating the policies of the government down to the servicemen and women. Even when the policy seems unfair or unreasonable the officer is required to represent the government's policy to his/her men and women with complete loyalty.[36] It could be, therefore, that the officer's concern for the welfare and morale of service personnel may well conflict with loyalty to the overall policy of the Armed Forces.

Further strain exists in this situation in that the pressures to conform are also intimately connected to the system of promotion. Although not quite reliant upon patronage, the confidential report system and through it the promotion system, are based upon the perceptions of an officer's superior of his subordinate's suitability for promotion. An officer who disturbs the status quo by representing more than the usual number of grievances may well jeopardise his/her chances of promotion. Thus, at an individual level, the system has within it in-built strains that work against effective representation upwards while still ensuring reliable downward communication of government policies. Representation at national level also has its problems.

The Armed Forces Pay Review Body[37] is an independent voluntary body that was established in 1972 to give advice on pay and allowances for all three services. Of its eight members only one is serving in the Armed Forces (presently Vice Admiral Sir Toby Frere KCB). Their remit is to ensure comparability between service and civilian pay while balancing the need to recruit and retain the right calibre of people against Government expenditure limits. To that end they take evidence each year from MoD, the services and other interested parties. As part of their research they visit servicemen and women to talk to them directly about pay and conditions. Last year they consulted 3,000 Service personnel and their spouses. However, there is no official mechanism for the collective concerns of servicemen and women to be represented to the Pay Review Body.

In contrast, the statutory body for negotiating police pay and terms of conditions is the Police Negotiating Board (PNB).[38] The PNB resulted from Section 61 of the Police Act (1996) which provided that there should be a body to consider:

> "Questions related to hours of duty, leave, pay and allowances, pensions or the issue and return of police clothing, personal equipment and accoutrements."[39]

There are two negotiating sides to the PNB, one representing the police authorities and the other representing members of the police forces. So, in this Board, all ranks of the police service are represented in negotiations by their respective Police Federations, Superintendents' Associations and Chief Police Officers' Staff Associations. The PNB exists to negotiate agreements which it recommends to the Home Secretary. Generally agreements are reached by a majority of both sides accepting a proposal.

However, in the event of a failure to agree within the PNB, matters (apart from pensions issues) can be referred to the Police Arbitration Tribunal whose awards are binding on both sides of the PNB. If the Home Secretary accepts the recommendations, they are placed within a draft statutory instrument (Police Regulations) and put to Parliament for approval. PNB agreements once placed in regulations are legally binding.

The disparities between the Armed Forces Pay Review system and the Police Negotiating Board are obvious, in the former, no collective negotiation is allowed and the recommendations are made by a non-representative body, whereas in the latter, police representatives from all ranks are an integral part of the statutory negotiating body that frames the recommendations.

The advantages of independent representation to servicemen and women are self-evident. In terms of individual representation a federation would be able to avoid the pitfalls of the chain of command and make direct representations at the highest level. This would also benefit officers lower down the chain of command who would no longer face the dilemma over the welfare of their subordinates or the prospects for promotion. At a national level, a system in which both sides discuss pay and conditions will not only allow for collective representation but will also be seen to be open and fair.

As well as benefiting servicemen and women such a system could also be of benefit to the MoD. Given that one of the lowest levels of satisfaction on the Army's Continuous Attitude Survey[40] is shown for pay and allowances, especially among junior soldiers and leavers, it might help recruitment, morale and retention if a system for pay negotiation between an 'official side' and a 'staff side' were introduced. Even if awards were constrained by government spending limits the negotiating system would be seen to be more representative than is presently the case. But, perhaps the most telling comment about representation was made by Gene Phillips in 1977:

> "Communications between management and workforce are at the heart of labor relations. They are at the heart of military leadership. Thus, [a representative] in a military unit... will be another legitimate means of communication. In this regard it will strengthen rather than usurp the chain of command."[41]

Legal

It is not the intention of this section to delve too deeply into the various legal systems of the three services which are complex and difficult to summarise. Suffice it to say that each service has its own scheme for legal support. In so far as service men and women are concerned the main purpose of military legal officers is to 'prosecute at courts-martial where the accused is normally represented by a civilian lawyer'.[42] The Army Legal Service also has a mandate to provide legal advice and assistance to service personnel where no other source of help is readily available. However, there are many situations affecting serving personnel in which they have no recourse to the kind of assistance in legal matters that would be available to members of trade unions or similar organisations. Some have been helped by pressure groups with a specific agenda but the majority have had to seek legal advice independently, often having to spend their own savings in order to defend themselves or to pursue claims.

This is a litigious society and it would not be in the interests of the Armed Forces to encourage further litigation. It has been argued, that a representative organisation would restrict the incidence of frivolous or malicious litigation by 'the self discipline that [it] could impose upon its members'.[43] Furthermore the malcontent and troublemaker would find no refuge in a military union or federation.

Nevertheless the fact is that MoD has a poor reputation when dealing with personnel issues. 'According to lawyers and campaign groups, the MoD routinely greets legal proceeding with incompetence, heavy-handedness, secretiveness and evasions.'[44] On average about 750 claims per year are now being brought against the MoD,[45] the majority of which are being funded either on a no-win-no-fee basis or out of the pockets of the claimants. These cases inevitably receive much publicity in the media and can only do harm to the reputation of the Armed Forces.

Independent representation could lead to claims being settled internally and not reaching court at all. This would be an advantage both to service personnel and the MoD. Furthermore, a responsible representative organisation could be of further use in 'flagging up' areas of concern so that the MoD is aware of the situation and would be in a position to remedy matters before they lead to court action.

There is also another disturbing development emanating from the European Convention on Human Rights. Unlike many European countries, Britain has not asked for its Armed Forces to be exempt from the convention. As a result, it is possible that officers could be sued by junior members of the Forces over orders they had given.[46] The government was less than positive when asked whether they would defend officers who were sued by junior members of the Forces. It would therefore seem possible that officers could be without any legal assistance if they are sued and might have to fund any defence from their own pockets. The Stankovic affair illustrates how this can happen[47] and highlights the need for an organisation that can provide legal assistance for officers and other ranks, something a Federation would do.

Discipline

The police, like the military, are subject to rules and are sometimes disciplined for breaking these rules. Minor transgressions are dealt with internally. Police officers will have the benefit of a Federation representative (if they should choose to have one) at any disciplinary hearing. Most disciplinary cases in the military are dealt with, in the first instance, by the Commanding Officer who has summary powers. Although it is possible for an accused to call for character witnesses during this summary procedure, there is no mechanism for representation nor an organisation that would provide such help at this level. The Commanding Officer can impose fines and even imprisonment upon those found to be guilty so it would be very advantageous for an accused to have recourse to the kind of help that is available to the police through the Federation.

Medical

Serving in the Armed Forces is a dangerous occupation and many members sustain injuries or contract illnesses through the execution of their duty. Some basic medical cover is available in Commands but the closure of the last military hospital has meant that servicemen and women are now reliant, in the main, upon the National Health Service. A number of major crises have occurred in the last ten years including the Gulf War Syndrome and the Depleted Uranium scare. Some of these have resulted in claims being made against the MoD for illnesses and injuries sustained through active service. While there is no doubt that the MoD does take care of those sick or injured in the line of duty, the system for investigating complicated claims for compensation is open to criticism.

The MoD can no longer rely on Crown Immunity to protect it from litigation and so it may have to shoulder responsibility for illness and injury suffered in places such as the Gulf, Bosnia and Sierra Leone.[48] It does have in-house mechanisms to investigate claims for injuries and illness but the slowness in reaching satisfactory conclusions has led many to seek independent medical advice and assistance.

Sufferers from Gulf War Syndrome, for example, have sought medical advice from specialists in America and Canada.[49] This has been at their own expense or with help from pressure groups such as the National Gulf Veterans and Families Association.

At present no official mechanism exists to help serving men and women to obtain independent medical advice and assistance to help them in making claims against the MoD. In contrast, the Police Federation have just such a system that provides money and medical examinations to support similar claims against the Police authorities.

The advantages to servicemen and women of a similar scheme are obvious but there are also possible advantages to the MoD. A reputable professional organisation would be able to filter out frivolous claims and also consolidate claims of a similar nature. Thus the MoD would have a single point of contact and also know that the claims had already been vetted and considered to be worth pursuing.

Personnel

In recent times the Armed Forces have made great strides in the development of a personnel strategy. The recently published Armed Forces Overarching Personnel Strategy[50] (AFOPS) has for the first time provided the three services with a comprehensive set of policies by which the progress of personnel developments can be measured. This is a welcome improvement. However, this document outlines Human Resource Management strategies at the macro level and much still needs to be done at the micro level in order to improve the poor reputation that the military have in personnel matters.[51]

Despite great strides being made by the Armed Forces in combating discrimination and bullying and championing equal opportunities, serious problems are still being highlighted.[52] The systems in place for reporting and identifying discrimination and bullying is very much dependent upon the determination of the individual being bullied or harassed and upon the chain of command. As well as the usual institutional inertia inherent within the chain of command, the MoD stands accused of being obstructive, often losing files, missing time limits and not furnishing all the facts.[53]

Furthermore, there are reported instances of service personnel running out of funds in pursuit of redress for harassment and bullying[54] with the result that the case has been sidelined. As in previous instances, it would benefit servicemen and women to have some representative body to take up individual cases and take them to a satisfactory conclusion. It would also benefit MoD to have reliable systems in place which ensure that the pursuit of those responsible for bullying and harassment is inevitable and successful.

Partnership

Inevitably there will be scepticism about any calls for independent representation in the Armed Forces. Whenever military unions are mentioned the old stories about Dutch troops wearing hairnets and not saluting are re-aired. Yet other more acceptable examples are conveniently forgotten. The German Army has had union representation for some time yet few would deny that it is an efficient and effective military organisation. What seems to be the problem as far as the military hierarchy is concerned is their lack of trust in servicemen and women to work for rather than against the organisation. They appear to see representation as a civilian employment practice that is 'entirely inappropriate for soldiers on the battlefield'.[55]

Yet it is possible for satisfactory partnerships to develop between employer and employees. For some years now the TUC has been working with industry to develop partnerships and this has resulted in it setting up a new organisation called the Partnership Institute.[56] Its rationale is that:

> "...partnership is the most effective approach to improve the working lives of trade union members and an essential element in any strategy to improve organisational performance. Partnership is rooted in the notion that mutual gains are possible even though unions and employers will inevitably have differences of interest from time to time."[57]

For such a partnership to develop there must exist a high level of trust between all participants. The TUC partnership scheme is based upon such a trust – that it is in the interests of both the employers and the employees for the organisation to succeed.

Most Armed Forces representative bodies seem to be based upon a similar level of trust. The Armed Forces Federation of Australia is one example. It came into existence in 1984 and has the full blessing of the hierarchy. The Chief of the Defence Force, Admiral Alan Beaumont, feels that 'The Federation's aim of protecting and promoting the welfare of its members is consistent with my objectives and those of the Chiefs of Staff.'[58]

People do not join the Armed Forces predominantly for money. Whatever their motives they are asked to be prepared to make the ultimate sacrifice. They are trusted with the arms and weapons that they need to defend the state. It does not seem logical that they cannot be trusted to organise in such a way as to protect and promote their own welfare. Ironically, the homosexual lobby group Rank Outsiders appears to have the trust of the MoD to promote a welfare and support network for gay and lesbian members of the Armed Forces. According to their Vice-Chairman they also have access to the highest levels within the MoD to represent their members.[59]

More paradoxically, when Radio Five wanted a representative from the ranks to talk about depleted uranium and lacking any alternative point of contact with other ranks, they asked Rank Outsiders to provide a spokesman.[60] The point being that if the MoD can trust a pressure group representing a small minority to act responsibly enough for them to have free access to both the media and the MoD hierarchy then they should be able to trust all their service personnel to behave just as sensibly. A partnership between the MoD and a Forces Federation could be a powerful force for initiating and managing change in the Armed Forces.

CONCLUSIONS

Of necessity this has been a brief look at some of the advantages to both service personnel and the MoD of independent representation. The underlying themes are about improving communication and redeveloping trust between senior officers (and MoD) and the remainder of the Armed Forces. Paternalism has had its day and servicemen and women want another system to replace it. Overwhelmingly, they have expressed a preference for some kind of representative body similar to the Police Federation with no mandate for any form of industrial action. Such an organisation could play a positive role in furthering and protecting the rights of service personnel in a number of areas.

Representation in pay negotiations, for example, would help to make the process more transparent, give voice to the views of the rank and file and perhaps stem the outflow of those lower ranks who are dissatisfied with the present pay structure. Access to legal advice and representation would be a major improvement to the present system in which many servicemen and women have to fight legal battles out of their own pockets. The Health and Safety at Work Act, for example, could well leave many open to legal action and an organisation that provides legal cover would allay the fears of many officers and NCOs on this matter.

Similarly, the introduction of representation at summary disciplinary hearings could be seen to be an improvement to a system that might be open to challenge under the Human Rights Act.

A 'Forces' Federation' could also provide a central focus for problems such as Gulf War Syndrome and depleted uranium. As well as providing medical advice and legal assistance to service personnel, such an organisation could also liaise with MoD to help to reconcile opposing points of view and perhaps reach a satisfactory conclusion to long-running medical controversies.

In personnel issues, as well, the military could benefit from the responsible assistance of a representative body. Most of the recent policy changes, admirable though they may be, have been made in isolation by civil servants and senior officers. An injection of views from the lower levels might well have helped to make the new policies more acceptable to the military as a whole.

But perhaps the most important contribution that independent representation could make would be to foster a new spirit of trust through the development of a partnership that unites all ranks.

The rise in support for independent representation appears to be based upon two major factors – communication and trust. While great strides are being made to improve downward communication what seems to be lacking at the moment is a satisfactory system of upward communication. The feeling seems to be that the chain of command cannot be relied upon as a means of passing information from the lower ranks to the senior officers or perhaps more to the point 'the chain of command are not prepared to fight for the interests of soldiers...they are too busy with budgets'.[61] Trust in the leadership seems to be at an all time low. Trust by the leadership does not seem to be any better, but 'unless the leadership is completely committed to creating an environment of trust...for *everyone* in the enterprise, nothing will change'.[62] A demonstration of trust in the Armed Forces to create a responsible representative body would go a long way towards remedying the present situation. After all it must be in the interests of the MoD to have 'content, loyal and motivated personnel to meet the requirements of defence policy'.[63]

NOTES

1. Bett M. *Independent Review of the Armed Forces' Manpower, Career and Remuneration Structures: Managing People in Tomorrow's Armed Forces*. London, HMSO, 1995.
2. Ibid. p.66.
3. See, for example: Bartle R. A. "The Army in the 21st Century – Addressing the Final Taboo?" *Royal United Services Institute Journal*, June 1998, pp.45–47. Bartle R. A. "Independent Representation in the Armed Forces", in Alexandrou A. and Bartle R. A. (eds.) *Human Resource Management in the Public Sector.* Cranfield University, RMCS, 1999. Chap. 2. Hill J. S. "Independent Representation for Servicemen – is it Desired, Desirable and Inevitable?" Unpublished MDA Dissertation. Cranfield University at RMCS. May 2000. Jenkins I. P. "Unionisation within the Military – An Anachronism or a Necessity?" Unpublished Defence Research Paper. Advanced Command and Staff Course No. 1, April 1998. Young M. A. 'Does the Army Need a Union?' Unpublished MDA Dissertation. Cranfield University at RMCS, December 1996.
4. *Queen's Regulations for the Army* (Revised 1995). London, HMSO (J12.019).
5. See Joyce E. S. "Tradition and Representation", *British Army Review*, No. 111, December 1995, and, Joyce E. S. "Arms and the man – Renewing the armed services", *Fabian Society*, August 1997.
6. "A chip on both epaulettes", *The Sunday Telegraph*, 17 January 1999.
7. "Armed Forces homosexual policy offends human rights", *The Times*, 11 October 1999.
8. Hollingworth C. "Will the ranks enlist in unions?" *The Telegraph*, Wednesday, 8 June 1977.
9. Bartle R. A. "The Army in the 21st Century – Addressing the Final Taboo?"

Royal United Services Institute Journal. June 1998, pp.45–47. Bartle R. A. "Can Independent Representation Remedy the Lack of Trust in the British Army?" in Rupert Tipples and Helen Shrewsbury (eds.) *Global Trends and Local Issues.* Proceedings of the Seventh International Employment Relations Conference, Canterbury, New Zealand. 1999, pp.49–62.

10. Reid J. "The Armed Forces and Society", *Royal United Services Institute Journal,* April 1997. pp.30–34.
11. McManners H. and Prescott M. "Robertson wins battle to deny troops minimum wage." *The Sunday Times,* 11 January 1998.
12. Convention for the Protection of Human Rights and Fundamental Freedoms http:// conventions.coe.int/treaty/EN/cadreprincipal.htm. p.10.
13. Ibid., p.10.
14. Bartle R. A. "Independent Representation in the Armed Forces", op. cit., p.19.
15. General Sir Michael Rose, quoted in McManners H. and Prescott M. "Robertson wins battle to deny troops minimum wage", *The Sunday Times,* 11 January 1998.
16. General Sir Roger Wheeler, Chief of the General Staff quoted in: *The Daily Telegraph.* "Duty must come before rights says Army chief", 18 February 1999.
17. For example see: Hill J. S. 'Independent Representation for Servicemen', op. cit. Jenkins I. P. 'Unionisation within the Military', op. cit. Young M. A. 'Does the Army Need a Union?', op. cit.
18. Webb B. and Webb S. *The History of Trade Unionism.*Longmans, 1920. Quoted in Taylor R. *The Future of the Trade Unions.* André Deutsch, 1994, p.4.
19. TUC written evidence to the House of Commons Select Committee Enquiry into Trade Unions 1993-94, quoted in: Taylor R. op. cit., p.5.
20. http://www.tuc.org.uk/pi/partnership.htm.
21. Bartle R. A. "The Army in the 21st Century" op. cit., pp.45–47.
22. Alexandrou A. 'The Police Federation of England and Wales', unpublished Briefing Paper, 1998.
23. Ibid. p.6.
24. Williams L. "Staff Representation within a Disciplined Service", unpublished paper, December 1999.
25. See, for example: Bartle R. A. "The Army in the 21st Century" op. cit., pp.45–47 and Young M. A. "Does the Army Need a Union?" op. cit.
26. Turner P. D. J. *Military Ethic as it applies to the Royal Air Force.* PMA/110004/26/Air Sec, October, 1997.
27. Glaister G. "Armed Forces and Unionisation", *Royal United Services Institute Journal,* June 1978. pp.61–66.
28. Bartle R. A. 'Can Independent Representation Remedy the Lack of Trust in the British Army?' op. cit. pp.49–62.
29. Joyce E. S. "Arms and the man" op. cit.
30. King T. Defence (Options for Change), in Hansard, 25 July 1990, cols. 468–486.
31. Welch J. "New Model Army". *People Management,* 4 December 1997, p.22.
32. Strachan H. (ed.) *The British Army, Manpower and Society into the Twenty-First Century.* London and Portland, OR, Frank Cass, 2000, p.xxii.
33. "Amputee soldier loses payout plea", *The Daily Telegraph,* 14 February 1999.
34. Joyce E. S. "Arms and the man", op. cit.
35. Bartle R. A. "The Army in the 21st Century" op. cit. pp.45–47.
36. Glaister G. op. cit. p.63.
37. http://www.mod.uk/data/[(1037)-11-06-2000]afpr2000.pdf.
38. http://www.lg-employers.gov.uk/stat_body.html.
39. Ibid.

40. Atherton R., Weston K., Wingfield T. and Thwaites S. *The Army Continuous Attitude Survey. Report Eleven.* DERA/CHS/MID/CR000043/1.0. February 2000.
41. Phillips G. "For a Brotherhood of Men-at-Arms: The Case for Military Unionization" in Sabrosky A. N. (ed.) *Blue Collar Soldiers? Unionization and the U.S. Military.* Westview Press, 1977.
42. http://www.army.mod.uk/army/organise/adjutant/main.htm#ALS.
43. Phillips G. op. cit. p. 63.
44. Lee D. "Battle Only the MoD Wins", *The Times*, Tuesday, 23 January 2001.
45. Ibid.
46. Bamber D. "Soldiers to be given right to sue their officers", *The Sunday Telegraph,* 27 February 2000.
47. http://trustedmole.org/index8.html
48. Lewis P. "A Dangerous Line of Work", *The Independent,* 20 February 2001.
49. National Gulf Veterans and Families Association. http://www. healthboards.com/gulf-war-syndrome/847.html.
50. Ministry of Defence. *Armed Forces Overarching Personnel Strategy.* MoD, London, February 2000.
51. Strachan H. op. cit. p.xxii.
52. Burke J. "Bullied army recruits being forced to desert", *The Observer,* 4 June 2000.
53. Lee D. "Battle only the MoD wins", *The Times, 23* January 2001.
54. Interview with officer, who for obvious reasons wishes to remain anonymous, 30 March 2001.
55. General Sir Michael Rose, quoted in McManners H. and Prescott M. "Robertson wins battle to deny troops minimum wage", *The Sunday Times,* 11 January 1998.
56. http://www.tuc.org.uk/pi/partnership.htm.
57. Ibid. p.1.
58. Averay T. "Unionisation in the Australian Armed Forces – The Emergence of the Armed Forces Federation of Australia", *Australian Defence Force Journal.* No.107, July/August 1994.
59. Interview with Simon Langley, Vice Chair Rank Outsiders, 23 January 2001.
60. Breakfast Show, Radio Five Live, Sunday 14 January 2001.
61. Bartle R. A. "Independent Representation in the Armed Forces." op. cit. Chapter 2.
62. Barrett R. quoted in Smith D. "Are Your Employees Bowling Alone? How to Build a Trusting Organization", *Harvard Management Update,* September 1998.
63. Jenkins I. P. "Unionisation within the Military" op. cit.

Index

Index

Index